SPORTS VENUE SECURITY: PUBLIC POLICY OPTIONS FOR SEAR 4–5 EVENTS

THIS PAGE INTENTIONALLY LEFT BLANK

THIS PAGE INTENTIONALLY LEFT BLANK

ABSTRACT

Although the United States made considerable advances in improving sport venue security following 9/11, many sporting events remain vulnerable to attack. The perceived lack of threat to smaller venues, budget limitations and technical constraints are restricting the level of patron and vehicle screening at Special Event Assessment Rating (SEAR) 4–5 events.

This thesis assesses the risk of attack by analyzing 21st century developments in explosive trace detection and closed-circuit television technologies, as well as trends surrounding the terrorist target value of SEAR 4–5 events. The research shows that these events have become viable, valuable terrorist targets because of increasing attendance and rapidly expanding exposure via cable television, satellite broadcasts, and the Internet. It identifies shortcomings of national protection doctrine and outlines potential cost-effective policy options to better support SEAR 4–5 sporting event venue security.

Establishing a national doctrine, organizational support and training standards, along with deploying select surveillance and detection technologies, will bring untold benefits to the national protection mission.

THIS PAGE INTENTIONALLY LEFT BLANK

TABLE OF CONTENTS

LIST OF FIGURES

THIS PAGE INTENTIONALLY LEFT BLANK

LIST OF TABLES

THIS PAGE INTENTIONALLY LEFT BLANK

LIST OF ACRONYMS AND ABBREVIATIONS

ACLU	American Civil Liberties Union
ACPO	Association of Chiefs of Police
AQAP	Al-Qaeda in the Arabian Peninsula
AS&E	American Science & Engineering, Inc.
ATSA	Aviation Transportation Security Act
BoL	Bureau of Labor
BSO	Black September Organization
BWI	Baltimore Washington International Airport
CBP	Customs and Border Protection
CCTV	closed circuit television (cameras)
CIA	Central Intelligence Agency
CNN	Central News Network
COF	Checkpoint of the Future
CPI	Consumer Price Index
CT	counterterrorism
DHS-OI	Department of Homeland Security, Office of Intelligence
DOD	Department of Defense
DoJ	Department of Justice
DHS	Department of Homeland Security
DTRA	Defense Threat Reduction Agency
E.U.	European Union
ESPN	Exclusively Sports Network
ETD	Explosive Trace Detection
FA	Football Association
FBI	Federal Bureau of Investigation
FEMA	Federal Emergency Management Agency
FLA	Football Licensing Authority
FIFA	Football International Federated Associations
FIO	football intelligence officer
FLO	football liaison officer
FY	fiscal year
GAO	Government Accountability Office

HQ	headquarters
HSE	Homeland Security Enterprise
HSGP	Homeland Security Grant Program
HSPD-8	Homeland Security Presidential Directive # 8
IATA	International Aviation Transport Association
IED	improvised explosive device
IRA	Irish Republican Army
JEVM	Journal of Event Venue and Management (U. of South Carolina)
JIEDDO	Joint Improvised Explosive Device Detection Office
JTTF	Joint Terrorism Task Force
KST	known or suspected terrorist
LE	law enforcement agency(ies)
MAJ	U.S. Army rank of major
MiLB	Minor League Baseball, Inc.
MLB	Major League Baseball, Inc.
MLS	Major League Soccer, Inc.
NaCTSO	National Counter Terrorism Security Office (U.K.)
NCAA	National Collegiate Athletic Association
NCIS	Naval Criminal Investigative Service (Television Program)
NCS4	National Center for Sport Spectator Safety and Security
NCTC	National Counter Terrorism Center (U.S.)
NGO	non-government organization
NIJ	National Institute of Justice
NIPP	National Infrastructure Protection Program
NPF	National Planning Framework
NPPD	National Protection and Planning Directorate (within DHS)
NSA	National Security Agency
NSSE	National Security Special Event
ODNI	Office of Director of National Intelligence
OGS	Office of Global Strategy
OKC	Oklahoma City (bombing)
PAC 12	Pacific Athletic Conference
PHASE	Photoacoustic Sensing of Explosives
PLO	Palestinian Liberation Organization
PPD-8	Presidential Policy Directive - Number 8
PTZ	point-tilt-zoom (CCTV cameras)
QHSR	Quadrennial Homeland Security Review

R&D	research and development
RBS	Risk-based Security
SAPIENT	E.U. Commissioned Working Group
SE	special event
SEAR	Special Event Assessment Rating
SEVT	Sports Entertainment Venues Tomorrow (at University of South Carolina)
SHSP	State Homeland Security Program
SL	state/local
SLLE	state/local law enforcement
SME	subject matter expert
SOC	security operations center
START	National Consortium for the Study of Terrorism and Responses to Terrorism
SUV	Sport Utility Vehicle
TSA	Transportation Security Administration
TSGP	Transportation Security Grant Program
U.K.	United Kingdom
UASI	Urban Area Security Initiative
UEFA	United European Football Association
UKFPU	United Kingdom Football Policing Unit
USG	U.S. government
UVF	Ulster Voluntary Force (N. Ireland)
WG	Working Group
yr	Year

THIS PAGE INTENTIONALLY LEFT BLANK

EXECUTIVE SUMMARY

The disparity in security at U.S. special events has left some venues more vulnerable to attacks via armed gunmen, suicide bombers, and improvised explosive devices. This difference in security priority is defined by each event's Special Event Assessment Rating (SEAR). SEAR 4–5 events, as softer targets than the SEAR 1–3 events, are less protected.

Despite scholarly and professional efforts to devise ways to prevent terror attacks, terrorism will certainly remain an effective strategic practice globally for many years to come, if not forever.[1] Furthermore, while communication technologies have brought the world closer, research reveals that 21st century globalization has benefitted those targeting the American Homeland.[2]

One such example of how the Internet can be used to cultivate radicalization in America involved *Inspire* online magazine. The bombers who carried out the attack during the 2013 Boston Marathon used instructions contained in the magazine's first issue to build and detonate their devices.[3] Countless other communication outlets share information about vulnerabilities in public event venue security. Even the basic use of cell phones can greatly facilitate complex attack coordination.[4] Considering these expansive communication factors, coupled with the ease of international travel

---

[1] John Mueller, "Six Rather Unusual Propositions about Terrorism," *Terrorism and Political Violence* 4, no. 17 (2005): 491, doi: 10.1080/095465591009359; United Kingdom Home Office, The United Kingdom's Strategy for Countering International Terrorism. Command Paper Number Cm 7547 (London: United Kingdom Home Office, March 24, 2009), 12, https://www.hsdl.org/?view&did=32602.

[2] Denise Lavoie and Tom Hays "Dzhokhar Tsarnaev, Boston Bombing Suspect, Was Influenced by Internet: Indictment," *Huffington Post,* June 28, 2013, http://www.huffingtonpost.com/2013/06/28/dzohkhar-tsarnaev-Internet-indictment_n_3515432.html.

[3] Bill McMahon in an interview with Edward Norris and Steve Davis on the "Norris and Davis Show," CBS, WJZ-FM, January 27, 2014, citing online instructions on how to use rudimentary explosives made from household goods like those that were found in the backpack of the lone attacker in the Columbia, MD, mall shooting on January 2014.

[4] Onook Oh, Agrawal Manish, and H. Raghav Rao, "Information Control and Terrorism: Tracking the Mumbai Terrorist Attack through Twitter," *Information Systems Frontiers* 14, no. 1 (March 2011): 33–43.

facilitating global integration, the United States can no longer rely on geographic isolation for security.

Even though astute, aggressive national counterterrorism (CT) strategy may prevent attacks in the homeland by foiling some plots in their earlier stages of development, there will remain unforeseen threats that will suddenly emerge to. Terrorists may arise from a wide variety of sources and not just from foreign, well-funded sub-nation state organizations.[5] Radicalized terrorists in the homeland present an extremely difficult threat to defend against because these attackers may be less susceptible to discovery by national intelligence and terrorist tracking sources.[6] Therefore, the last line of CT security will always need to be on-site at the intended "ground-zero" target location of an event.[7]

As a result, the Homeland Security Enterprise (HSE) must remain agile to quickly adapt to evolving terrorist strategies and choices of target and be vigilant in its campaign to seek improvement and transition over time to provide protection from terrorist attacks in the homeland.[8]

This thesis analyzes the current threat to sporting events and the status of venue security to assess and identify potential needs for cost-effective public policy evolutions to better protect SEAR 4–5 events from terrorist attacks.[9]

The analysis was structured to answer three primary research questions:

- How well is the current National Protection Mission policy framework (the status quo) providing counterterrorism protection at sporting events in

---

[5] Bruce Hoffman, "Defending America against Suicide Terrorism," in *Three Years After: Next Steps in the War on Terror*, edited by David Aaron, 21–24 (Santa Monica, CA: RAND, 2005), 9.

[6] Billy Kenber, "Nidal Hasan Convicted of Ft. Hood Killings," *Washington Post*, August, 23, 2013; Lavoie and Hays, "Dzhokhar Tsarnaev."

[7] U.S. Department of Homeland Security (DHS), *Quadrennial Homeland Security Review Report: A Strategic Framework for a Secure Homeland* (Washington, DC: DHS, February 2010), 1; U.S. National Counterterrorism Center (NCTC) *2011 Report on Counterterrorism* (Washington, DC: DHS, March 2012), 13.

[8] *Homegrown Terrorism: The Threat to Military Communities Inside the United States: Hearing before the Committee on Homeland Security,* 112th Cong., 1st sess., (2011).

[9] The term "cost-effective" will be used to express the concept to field surveillance/detection technologies or new doctrinal practices to at little cost, or innovatively funded to meet larger cost courses of action.

light of a) increasing publicity and exposure through global media coverage at SEAR 4–5 events, and b) more rigorous protection at SEAR 1–3 event?

- Are there quantitative or qualitative methods to demonstrate a positive cost-benefit relationship between potential solutions versus consequential alternatives?

- If evolution in security for SEAR 4–5 events is needed, what cost-effective public policy solutions can be synthesized into a better Counterterrorism protection paradigm?

The Department of Homeland Security Risk Management Framework provided in the National Infrastructure Protection Plan (NIPP) establishes the steps to combine consequence, vulnerability, and threat information to generate an assessment of national or sector risk. The national objective is to weigh infrastructure security priorities, goals, and requirements to allocate security resources effectively in order to reduce vulnerability, deter threats, and minimize the consequences of attacks.[10] With the NIPP model as the larger framework, the concepts used to construct the analytical framework in this thesis were derived from a thorough review of the literature on terrorist psychology, security technology, comparative security, and cost-benefit analysis formula and theory.

The first question is answered with analysis in four parts: data trends in terrorism attacks; the effects of increased security at SEAR 1–3 events; the effects of no requisite or licensing-based security metric; and the rapid, 21st century evolution of global sports broadcasting in real-time. Quantitative data such as patron attendance, media exposure to sporting events, and SEAR 4–5 events data were examined. Qualitative comparison was employed and examined doctrinal gaps and potential vulnerabilities that were revealed in the baseline literature review and public policies. The qualitative review also analyzed the gaps in the current HSE organizational structure, especially using comparative analysis of the experience of other nations. Adding to this, data reflect that the mega-events are spending immense amounts of money and committing vast numbers of security personnel to pose a much more difficult challenge for terrorists to penetrate than

---

[10]Georgios Giannopoulos, Roberto Filippini, and Muriel Schimmer, *Risk Assessment Methodologies for Critical Infrastructure Protection: Part I, A State of the Art* (Luxembourg: Publications Office of the European Union, 2012), 34–35.

ever before. Meanwhile, similar or greater casualty rates are attainable at the soft target venues. Coupled with the tremendously rapid increase of national and global coverage of SEAR 4–5 events in real-time (such as NFL, MLB, MiLB or NCAA athletic events), from the terrorists' perspective, the phenomenon of displacement is worthy of grave consideration, transforming these SEAR 4–5 venues into attractive targets.

The purpose of the second research question is to examine an objective means of weighing a cost-benefit analysis in order to determine grounds for the affordability of public policy action and respond to opposition of new forms of HSE expenditure. Using the cost-benefit analysis formula established in *Terror, Security, and Money*, the thesis has demonstrated that there are quantifiable methods to adjudicate and deem select expenditures as worthy and pragmatic.[11]

The scenario used was a successfully orchestrated, simultaneous, geographically dispersed multiple IED attack at four respective venues. The full range of costs to American society resulting from a catastrophic terrorist attack at a SEAR 4–5 sports venue is summarized in Table 1:

One-time Damages	Subsequent Annual Damages
Value of Lives (Quantified by Mueller)	Subsequent Enhancements Instituted
Liability for Injuries	Ticket Sales
Facility Property Damage	Club Revenues Future Losses
Corollary Property (Adjacent Buildings)	Marketing Ad Losses
Response, Rescue, & Clean Up	Area Economic Disruption Activity
Reconstruction	Businesses Bankrupt As Result

Table 1.   Successful Attack Cost Factors[12]

---

[11] John Mueller and Mark G. Stewart, *Terror, Security, and Money: Balancing the Risks, Benefits, and Costs of Homeland Security* (Oxford, UK: Oxford University Press, 2011).

[12] Ibid; Claude Journès, "Policing and Security: Terrorists and Hooligans," *Sport in Society* 1, no. 2 (1998): 145–60.

However, for the purposes of the cost-benefit demonstration, basing the success of such an attack on the quantified value of lives lost, alone, demonstrated that there is a reasonable break-even point at which federal public policy action should be taken. Considering the massive costs of all the factors together only further substantiates the benefit of select cost-effective public policy actions.

In answering the third research question, it was revealed that the sports entertainment industry may be one of the few business sectors in America that public policy action can be teamed with the private sector as well as with resource input from the patrons to share in the costs of providing solutions. There are current models of government-private sector cooperation that also include the customer-citizens to establish forms of "voluntary taxes," or funding for government coordinated projects. For example, the U.K. has set up the Football Foundation, and within the U.S., the TSA serves as such a model.

Upon thorough analysis, the findings produce new considerations regarding the feasibility of direct government involvement, the indirect provision of government incentives, or as an alternative, the possible existence of other low-cost, advantageous courses of action for SEAR 4–5 sporting events. As a result, ideas both innovative and revisited are presented for HSE consideration and potential working group research and development.

The overarching conclusion of this thesis is the necessity for the federal government and private sector to build an exceptionally robust public-private collaboration to more successfully protect SEAR 4 and 5 sports venues from potential terrorist attacks. The following recommendations provide a viable range of options, which when implemented in full, will affect this partnership and strengthen existing security measures at these less nationally prominent yet vulnerable venues.

The recommendations of this thesis are listed in order of escalating cost and associated with increasing legislative and/or public resistance. The final recommendation, however, is in preparation for the future and involves no current fiscal expense. Provided here is a summary list of the recommendations with the lead agency/entity denoted; each recommendation is subsequently explained in greater detail:

1. Finalize and publish the National Protection Framework with a specified annex for sporting event venue security (DHS)

2. Establish a streamlined office within HSE for inspection and compliance adherence (DHS)

3. Replicate U.K.'s organizational structure placing a federal Subject Matter Expert with state/local level personnel to synchronize security at the local level with the national level to improve operational harmonization (DHS)

4. Allocate 2.2% of the FEMA Grant budget annually for a five year plan dedicated to reduce security vulnerabilities at SEAR 4–5 venues nationwide (DHS)

5. Assess a statutory security fee on sporting event ticket purchases to fund enhanced SEAR 4–5 venue security, while acting to obtain patron stakeholder partnership with the government (DHS and Congress)

6. Create a charitable foundation to serve as a funding source dedicated to stadium infrastructure renovations to facilitate improved security for SEAR 4–5 events (private sector)

7. Rapidly prepare for future use of CCTV facial recognition technology by addressing operational and legal concerns immediately (DHS)

In order to render these recommendations a reality, several steps are necessary in the near term and long term future.

The first step is for DHS to form a Working Group across department and agency borders. It is essential to remove the idea of such creative solutions from the abyss of the federal stove-pipe syndrome, where ideas are thought of and conceived simultaneously but without coordination (i.e., repeating the same efforts and wasting time and resources in so doing).

This Working Group (WG) should examine the nuances of the issues raised and further research the shaping of the thesis recommendations. The WG will also bear the responsibility and authority to form a collective judgment not only regarding doctrinal revisions and additions, but for deriving new HSE organizational structures and working relationships, assessing technological capabilities, and laying the groundwork for the innovative funding streams recommended. These actions would tremendously serve the people by evaluating and planning for the future development of where, when, and how to stop terrorist attacks in America.

The WG must be expansive enough to be insightful but not bloated to the point of inaction or inability to move at anything more than glacial speed. Preparations are needed now for technology innovations on the cusp of becoming reality in the market. More importantly, as facility managers already perceive, it is just a matter of time before attacks occur at SEAR 4–5 venues. The WG must move forward with purpose. Therefore, representation on the WG will be needed from:

- Professional sports league Security Directors from MLB, NFL, NBA, NHL, and MLS;

- Three select NCAA Security Directors, such as one each from the Southeastern Conference, the Big 10, and the Pac 12;

- The state/local law enforcement community, such as the Association of Chiefs of Police, several major metropolitan Police Chiefs such as from New York, Boston, and Dallas, as well as a few select State Police Chiefs;

- Federal law enforcement SMEs from the FBI and JTTF;

- Intelligence Community representation, i.e., one or two SMEs from any of ODNI, NSA, CIA, DHS-OI and/or NPPD;

- The Academic community, with a representative from the two leading centers for sports venue security study at the University of South Carolina and Southern Mississippi University

A WG of these 18–20 representatives with DHS HQ synchronization will serve as an excellent resource base of Subject Matter Expertise and be reflective of an industry-wide partnership with the HSE.

Though the thesis recommendations may incur some modicum of cost for the most ambitious applications, the WG can fully analyze the investment for long-term security.

Because even state and local agencies in the U.S. are facing austere fiscal climates, the burden of the training for local law enforcement and private sector security teams can be shared with the federal government. The WG can advocate congressional action to grant private sector incentives, statutory fees, and FEMA funding for training venue security team employees how to use world class technology and to conduct training to standard in the roles as emergency first responders, as is done in the U.K. Such funding for training can be used by DHS for conferences and forums that continue to push constantly developing technology and collaboration in the security industry. With such equipment and SOC precision planning possible, the security workforce executing the operations plans must receive comparable quality training.

The WG will also serve as the initial collaborative planning body for the operational partnership between federal and state/local levels. It will establish the roles and responsibilities for the federal embedded personnel and make determinations as to where these people will work daily, such as at fusion centers or in police departments. The WG can also complete detailed reviews of other functional and logistically practical aspects of implementation.

So it is imperative that DHS establish the Working Group to explore the possibilities recommended in this thesis, to ensure the HSE is making its fullest effort to accomplish its Homeland Security protection mission.

Just because a well-orchestrated, multiple coordinated IED attack has not yet reigned catastrophe at America's smaller sports venues, does not mean that the United States government should not take prudent, sage steps forward to prepare a defense for that imminent terrorist strategy. The NCTC considers this a worst case scenario, and so too should DHS.

If the Department of Homeland Security is to win not only in the close-in, current battle against terrorism, but also in the deep, future battle against terrorism as well, then it must take time to recognize the status-quo of its protection mission posture as insufficient to meet the threat of an ever-increasingly more sophisticated enemy. Such status-quo recognition will illuminate where increased protection is needed today and paths forward tomorrow. DHS should proactively pursue and act on the recommendations provided in this thesis by establishing a professional Working Group to improve on the HSE protection mission of sports venues today and move aggressively into the future, before the enemy does.

ACKNOWLEDGMENTS

He who destroys a life, it is as if had destroyed an entire world;
He who saves a life, it is as if he had saved an entire world.

—Babylonian Talmud Tractate Sanhedrin 37 A

I want to extend thanks to many people, but most of all, to my wife, Kerrin. Thank you, Kerrin, for your endless patience with me and your enormous capacity to give of yourself. Your intellectual depth and breadth works amid a spectrum of political, sociological, psychological, and spiritual trains of thought and concepts as skillfully and artistically as one of the great renaissance masters wielding colors or clay.

Your heart, soul, and tireless patience have made my academic, professional, and personal journey in life a joy, and you have made it complete.

It is with immense gratitude that I acknowledge the scores of others, without whom, this academic vision could not have happened:

- To my thesis advisors, Paul Smith and Dr. Chris Bellavita: Thank you for your tremendous support and encouragement advocating creative thought, realistic research, and true standards of excellence for professional expression. I appreciate you encouraging me to not just write this thesis, but to strive to make it great. You've inspired me to consider a future career in academics. If I can play but a small part in making the collective great, then that is my having achieved the goal. Thank you, Paul, for devoting an extraordinary amount of time and premier effort to show me how to think clearly and keep me from getting "the Blues."

- To Dr. Chris Bellavita and Dr. Anders Strindberg: Thank you for rekindling in me a fervent desire to learn, and opening my eyes and my mind to find creative, spiritually reflective, and inspired thought. Your exceptional intellectual gifts will be my model to emulate for many years to come.

- To the first-ever Chief of the National Guard Bureau to serve on the Joint Chiefs of Staff, General Frank Grass: Thank you for your lifetime's example to me, both as my mentor and professional leader in war. You showed me what it is to devote a life to serving this country and to tirelessly persist to overcome any obstacle.

- To Command Sergeant Major Roger Haller, Staff Sergeant Daniel Suplee, Colonel Paul Johnson, and the first young Army soldier whose National Guard unit I selected to go to Afghanistan and who did not return home: To all of you my Brothers in Arms, your life lived and your ultimate sacrifice for all of us is the reason America has been alive for 238 years, and it is the reason I continue on in the Homeland Security profession.

- To my departed friends, Jenny Elwood and Dawn Mirenzi: Thank you for your inspirational courage in the face of cancer while you were here on Earth, showing me that bravery is not only confined to the battlefield.

- To Edmund Burke, President Ronald Reagan, Dr. W. Ross Yates, and Dr. Barbara Tuchman: Thank you for your roles in history, illuminating my academic life, and for furthering the cause of mankind's philosophical thought and wisdom.

- To Jose S. Chaves, Transportation Security Administration; David Warner, London Metropolitan Police; Jim Ammons, Federal Bureau of Investigation; Don McKinnon, Department of Homeland Security; Lawrence Rabalais, Louisiana State University; Don Paisant, New Orleans Superdome; Dr. Tom Regan, University of South Carolina; Dr. Geoff Alpert, University of South Carolina; and Dr. Kathleen Kiernan, Naval Postgraduate School: Thank you all for your priceless firsthand insights and tremendous contributions to my research.

- To Keith Malley and Sam Mumley, Transportation Security Administration: Thank you for your time, endless encouragement, and invaluable support opening this door of opportunity for me.

- To my father and mother, Harry and Betty Gehring, and to Gregory Gehring, Mark and Elisabeth Fordney: Thank you for giving me encouragement, a work ethic, and common sense to think outside the box.

- To my departed mother, Betty: I am especially thankful. You were the rock and foundation of courage, wisdom, and intellectual curiosity in all of our lives. You showed me that intelligence and wisdom does not come from a classroom, and that love of academic pursuit comes from the heart.

- Praise be to God, the Most Merciful: I thank Him for boundless benevolence, divine wisdom, and endless mercy; and to God incarnate, the Messiah, a real man named Jesus of Nazareth.

All of them have led me to see what I have seen, to think what I think, and to say what I say.

I. INTRODUCTION

A man full of warm, speculative benevolence may wish his society otherwise constituted than he finds it, but a good patriot and a true politician always considers how he shall make the most of the existing materials of his country. A disposition to preserve and an ability to improve, taken together, would be my standard of a statesman.

—Edmund Burke,
Reflections on the Revolution in France

With American sporting events numbering into the tens of thousands annually at more than 1,350 sports arenas and stadiums in the U.S., viable, valuable, and vulnerable terror targets abound on a daily basis.[1] The National Counterterrorism Center (NCTC) asserts that improvised explosive device (IED) attacks yield the highest casualties of any form of terror attack, and multiple coordinated IED attacks are of paramount concern for operations planning.[2] This kind of attack was carried out during the 2013 Boston Marathon, and the bombers used instructions contained in the first issue of the online magazine *Inspire* to build and detonate their devices. The guide was called "Make a bomb in the kitchen of your mom."[3] *Inspire* is produced by Al Qaeda in the Arabian Peninsula (AQAP), has been linked to terrorist cases, and contains exhortations to carry out "lone wolf" terrorist attacks by radicalized homegrown groups and individuals. Al Qaeda-linked websites are believed to have more than 100,000 registered members worldwide.[4] Homeland Security Enterprise (HSE) practitioners, planners, and senior leaders, all striving to protect the public, need to expediently address the 21st century's rapidly changing factors exacerbating the vulnerability of America's public sporting event venues.

---

[1] "Intercollegiate Athletics Summit." National Center for Spectator Sports Safety and Security (NCS4). January 2014. https://www.ncs4.com/summit/overview.

[2] U.S. National Counterterrorism Center (NCTC) 2011 NCTC *Report on Counterterrorism* (Washington, DC: NCTC, March 2012), 9.

[3] Stephen Wright, "Were They Inspired by Al Qaeda Magazine? Authorities Investigating Whether Terrorists Were Spurred Into Action by Publication Which Urges 'Lone Wolf' Attacks." *MailOnline*, May 22, 2013. http://www.dailymail.co.uk/news/.

[4] Ibid.

1

The vast majority of the scope and plethora of these terrorism targets are outside of the fortified confines of the most high profile, widely publicized events such as the Super Bowl or the Olympics. These sports mega-events have been historically perceived as primed for terrorists to send a worldwide message by executing an attack during the broadcast, potentially reaching tens of millions of viewers simultaneously across the globe. However, these mega-events are routinely designated by the American Homeland Security Enterprise (HSE) as either National Security Special Events (NSSE) or as special events (SE).

Of these HSE designations, the NSSEs and the highest rated of the SEs bring greatly enhanced security from sizable federal resources rendering them virtual fortresses to withstand any terrorist plot to strike them. Therefore, security for these events is not the subject of this thesis but will be reviewed and analyzed to establish a contextual framework of the status quo security provided to lower rated SEs. This framework will also shed light on the challenges faced by the security community whose mission it is to protect the lower-rated SEs. Essentially, the subject of the thesis is that as the NSSEs and highest-rated SEs have become more secure, the lower priority SEs have become more vulnerable.

Though historically regarded as less worthy to terrorists, these lower-rated SEs are the targets that are widely acknowledged as easier to strike, constituting them as "soft targets." If struck with lethality and simultaneous multiplicity, in the manner of a strategically audacious but foreseeable attack like 9/11,[5] then a terrorist cause will draw great attention to its policy goals and to the vulnerability in the everyday life of our society here in the U.S., instilling fear in Main Street, USA.

A.   STATEMENT OF THE PROBLEM

There will be terrorists in the homeland, either from abroad, lone wolf, or homegrown radicals; there is a disparity in the amount of security support provided between Special Event Assessment Rated (SEAR) 1–3 (higher priority) events and SEAR

---

[5] U.S. National Commission on Terrorist Attacks Upon the United States (9/11 Commission), *The 9/11 Commission Report* (Washington, DC: U.S. Government Printing Office, July 22, 2004).

4–5 events; and the SEAR 4–5 events being softer targets than the SEAR 1–3 events are more vulnerable to attack from armed gunmen, suicide bombers, and various IED attacks.

Despite scholarly and professional efforts to understand the motives of terrorists in order to devise ways to prevent terror attacks, terrorism will certainly remain an effective strategic practice globally for many years, if not forever.[6] With communication technologies advancing to bring the world closer, research reveals that 21st century globalization has benefitted those targeting the American Homeland.[7] *Inspire* magazine is one such example of how the Internet can be used to cultivate radicalization in America. In addition to online instructions on producing and using bombs, there are countless other forums to seek out and share information about vulnerabilities in public event venue security.[8] Furthermore, even the basic use of cell phones can greatly facilitate complex attack coordination.[9] Considering these expansive communications factors, coupled with the ease of international travel facilitating global integration, the United States can no longer rely on geographic isolation for security.

Even though astute, aggressive national counterterrorism (CT) strategy may prevent attacks in the homeland by foiling some plots in their earlier stages of development, there will remain unforeseen threats that will suddenly emerge. Terrorists may arise from a variety of sources and not just from foreign, well-funded sub-nation state organizations.[10] Radicalized terrorists in the homeland present an extremely difficult threat to defend because these attackers may be less susceptible to discovery by

6 John Mueller, "Six Rather Unusual Propositions about Terrorism," *Terrorism and Political Violence* 4, no. 17 (2005): 487–505. doi: 10.1080/095465591009359.

7 Denise Lavoie and Tom Hays "Dzhokhar Tsarnaev, Boston Bombing Suspect, Was Influenced by Internet: Indictment," *Huffington Post,* June 28, 2013,

.8 Bill McMahon in an interview with Edward Norris and Steve Davis on the "Norris and Davis Show," CBS, WJZ-FM, January 27, 2014, citing online instructions on how to use rudimentary explosives made from household goods like those that were found in the backpack of the lone attacker in the Columbia, MD, mall shooting on January 25, 2014.

9 Onook Oh, Agrawal Manish, and H. Raghav Rao, "Information Control and Terrorism: Tracking the Mumbai Terrorist Attack through Twitter," *Information Systems Frontiers* 14, no. 1 (March 2011): 33–43.

10 Bruce Hoffman, *Inside Terrorism* (New York: Columbia University Press, 2006), 9.

national intelligence and terrorist tracking sources.[11]   Therefore, the last line of CT security will always need to be on-site at the intended "ground-zero" target location of an event.[12]

As a result, the HSE must remain agile to quickly adapt to evolving terrorist strategies and choices of target. It must be vigilant in its campaign to seek improvement and transition over time to provide protection from terrorist attacks in the homeland.[13]

This thesis analyzes the current threat to sporting events and the status of venue security to assess and identify potential needs for cost-effective public policies to better protect SEAR 4–5 events from terrorist attacks.[14]

B.   BACKGROUND AND NEED

For background, it is requisite to specify that the NSSE designation merits the most amount of federal support, which includes federal funding, equipment, and personnel from various agencies in the HSE. Routinely, there are only a handful of these NSSEs declared annually. If a SE does not merit the NSSE rating, it is rated from 1 to 5 in descending order of security risk and therefore, priority for attention and support. These SE security ratings are designated as Special Event Assessment Ratings (SEAR).

The SEs that are designated with the highest three tiers of status, SEAR 1–3, also receive federally provided equipment and personnel in varying degrees, but unlike the NSSEs, they receive no direct federal funding. For example, the NFL Super Bowl is a SEAR 1 event and receives voluminous equipment and personnel from across multiple federal agencies for support. SEAR 2–3 events, such as the Boston Marathon and the Coca-Cola 600, respectively, also receive federal support, but on reducing scales.

---

11 Billy Kenber, "Nidal Hasan Convicted of Ft. Hood Killings," *Washington Post*, August, 23, 2013; Lavoie and Hays, "Dzhokhar Tsarnaev."

12 U.S. Department of Homeland Security (DHS), *Quadrennial Homeland Security Review Report: A Strategic Framework for a Secure Homeland* (Washington, DC: DHS, February 2010), 1; NCTC, *2011 NCTC Report on Counterterrorism* (Washington, DC: NCTC, March 2012), 13.

13 *Homegrown Terrorism: The Threat to Military Communities Inside the United States: Hearing before the Committee on Homeland Security,* 112th Cong., 1st sess., (2011).

14 The term "cost-effective" will be used to express the concept to field surveillance/detection technologies or new doctrinal organization and practices at little cost, or innovatively funded to meet larger cost courses of action.

However, there exist many more SEAR 4 and 5 sporting events than SEAR 1–3 events. These SEAR 4 and 5 events are considered to have limited national importance or may be of some national recognition with only local or state importance.[15] Major League Baseball regular season games and select NCAA Division I football games are considered SEAR 4 events. Accordingly, Minor League Baseball games and most NCAA Division I football and basketball games will constitute SEAR 5 ratings.[16]

Level 1	• Significant national and/or international importance • May require extensive federal interagency support	• NFL Super Bowl • United Nations General Assembly
Level 2	• Significant events with national and/or international importance • May require some national-level support	• Boston Marathon • DC Fourth of July • NY New Year's Eve • Kentucky Derby
Level 3	• Events of national and/or international importance • Require only limited federal support	• Coca-Cola 600 • Rolling Thunder • Oklahoma State Fair
Level 4	• Limited national importance • Handled at the state and local level	• Major League Baseball Games • NCAA Division I Football Games (e.g., Big 10 Football Championship)
Level 5	• Events that may be nationally recognized but generally have local or state importance	• Minor League Baseball Games • NCAA Division I Football and Basketball Games

Table 1.   Special Event Assessment Rating (SEAR) Categories[17]

The need for perpetually reviewing venue security and weighing improvements emanates from the sports entertainment industry, which, as one of the largest industries in America, captures close to two-thirds of the world's $700 billion annual sport industry revenues.[18] Yet the sporting event industry is not only a significant part of the American economy but is also a prominent fixture in the American social fabric. Because sporting events warrant a tremendous level of advertising, strong links of support from alcohol producers, and flashy displays by female cheerleaders, an attack on such a venue can support a vehement cultural judgment assailing American societal values. These venues,

---

15 U.S. Department of Homeland Security (DHS). Office of Operations Coordination and Planning (OPS), Special Events Program (SEP) and Special Events Working Group (SEWG): Program Overview and Federal Coordination Team Briefing (Washington, DC: DHS, January 2014).

16 Ibid.

17 Ibid.

18 Patrice Zygband and Hervé Collignon, "The Sports Market," *A.T. Kearney,* May 2011. http://www.atkearney.com/paper/-/asset_publisher/dVxv4Hz2h8bS/content/the-sports-market/10192.

therefore, serve as ideological targets as well as economic targets at which to inflict injury, death, and destruction. An attack against these SEAR 4–5 events will readily make a strong cultural statement to Americans.

Furthermore, sporting events permit millions and millions of Americans to retreat from the anxiety of their day-to-day challenges in life to a protected haven of emotional outlet. Like other forms of public entertainment, sporting events possess a cornerstone of trust and safety with the American public.[19] A successful attack on such a haven can send a strong strategic message to the American public that the terrorists will not rest, and they will reach Americans in their trusted sanctuaries. Such a strike can signal that terrorist organizations are more pervasive and more powerful in the homeland than previously considered. These messages are extremely persuasive to demonstrate to the American people that the terrorist cause is not worth contesting at the national strategic or diplomatic level.[20]

Meanwhile, there is no consistent national standard for all five SEAR ratings regarding technologies employed, doctrinal practices, and training, and the state of the public-private stakeholder collaborative enterprise management.[21] This is a key shortfall that is reminiscent of the pre-9/11 aviation transportation industry, and is therefore an urgent issue which this thesis will address.

Following the successful terrorist attacks in 2001, the 9/11 Commission assessed that the multiple security contract companies and each respective airline's security capabilities "failed utterly" to prevent the 19 terrorists from on-boarding aircraft with very basic lethal weapons.[22] The attackers "defeated all of the security layers that America's civil aviation security system had in place."[23] The commission found the

---

19 Kristine Toohey, "Terrorism, Sport and Public Policy in the Risk Society," *Sport in Society* 11, no. 4 (2008): 429–42. doi: 10.1080/17430430802019367.

20 Toohey, "Terrorism," 433.

21 Stacey Hall, Lou Marciani, Walter Cooper, and Robert Rolen, "Securing Collegiate Sport Stadiums in the 21st Century: Think Security, Enhance Safety," *Homeland Security Institute, Journal of Homeland Security* (August 2007). https://www.hsdl.org/?view&did=30643.

22 9/11 Commission, *The 9/11 Commission Report,* 4.

23 Ibid., 4.

different standards of security conducted by the varying contract companies associated with their respective airlines as a significant cause of the security failure.[24] This thesis will analyze how America's sporting venue security eerily possesses some of the same inconsistent qualities as that of pre-9/11 aviation transportation with no set national doctrine or standards for equipment deployment, personnel training, or operational management.

In the immediate aftermath of the September 2001 attacks, there arose many organizationally driven security precautions at sporting events nationwide. However, within six months, these heightened security measures were increasingly seen as problematic to venue and event managers.[25] In the ensuing years, facility managers, professional team ownership groups, and college administrations worked to provide security at public events, but with this success, came a sense of complacency.[26] By 2011, only one third of the 1,350 sports arenas and stadiums in the U.S. were providing heightened security measures compared to those that were in place in the 1990s.[27]

Notwithstanding the attention to the pre-emptive activity to interdict plots as far from the target site as possible, there still exists the possibility that terrorists will emerge at venues with little or no advance notice to the event security teams on location.[28] These enemies may be members of well-organized terror cells, radicalized homegrown extremists, or "lone wolf" attackers.

Therefore, this thesis will focus on the threat of suicide bombers, attackers using IEDs, and armed gunmen targeting any of America's SEAR 4–5 rated public sporting venues. The thesis will consider the terrorist that has defeated or otherwise bypassed the many layers of the HSE attempting to detect and interdict them before arriving at the

---

24 Ibid., 3.

25 Ronald E. Hurst, Catherine Pratsinakis, and Paul H. Zoubek, "American Sports As a Target of Terrorism: The Duty of Care after September 11th," *Martindale.com*, May 1, 2003, http://www.martindale.com/legal-library/Article_Abstract.aspx?an=entertainment-sports&id=2342.

26 Hurst, Pratsinakis, and Zoubek, "American Sports."

27 Peter Keating, "Industry of Fear," *ESPN The Magazine*, September 11, 2011, http://espn.go.com/espn/story/_/id/6936819/stadiums-increase-budgets-heighten-security-measures-protect-fans-espn-magazine.

28 For example, the Tsarnaev brothers' successful bombing of the 2013 Boston Marathon.

sporting event venue. The primary concern of the thesis is the last line of counterterrorism defense, at the venue.

C.   RESEARCH QUESTIONS

This thesis will establish three primary research questions:

- How well is the current National Protection Mission policy framework (the status quo) providing counterterrorism protection at sporting events in light of a) increasing publicity and exposure through global media coverage at SEAR 4–5 events, and b) more rigorous protection at SEAR 1–3 event?

- Are there quantitative or qualitative methods to demonstrate a positive cost-benefit relationship between potential solutions versus consequential alternatives?

- If evolution in security for SEAR 4–5 events is needed, what cost-effective public policy solutions can be synthesized into a better counterterrorism protection paradigm?

D.   SIGNIFICANCE OF RESEARCH TO THE HOMELAND SECURITY ENTERPRISE

This research aims to assess the potential for terrorist attacks at single or multiple coordinated SEAR 4–5-rated sporting events, and if necessary or possible, what may be cost-effective possibilities for public policy consideration. There has been literature published and various sports organizational efforts to move at the local level to increase threat awareness, recognition of venue security vulnerability, and improved collaboration for user-level best practices.[29] However, these efforts have been largely independent of each other with little centralized visibility, synchronization, or support. Additionally, there has been modest noteworthy research at the strategic level to determine possible next steps for a federal role to support the solidification of the nation's CT homeland defense at SEAR 4–5 sporting events nationwide.

---

29 Gary Joseph Lhotsky, "An Analysis of Risk Management at NCAA Division I-A Football Stadiums," Paper 3082 (PhD diss., Florida State University, 2005). http://diginole.lib.fsu.edu/cgi/viewcontent.cgi?article=3016&context=etd

This thesis will be especially of interest to stakeholders involved in the venue security paradigm. In particular, the framework provided may assist in shaping policy for three main constituencies:

- Those in the respective sporting industries—such as the professional sporting leagues (e.g., the NFL, MLB, Minor League Baseball [MiLB]; the collegiate sporting organizations at the national and regional levels, including the NCAA, the Southeastern Conference, the Big 10).

- American government policy makers—such as at the federal level (e.g., Congress, the Department of Homeland Security, Department of Justice, Intelligence Community agencies); at the state and local (SL) level(e.g., legislatures and mayor's offices, state and metropolitan police, state rapid and mass transit authorities, state offices of business development and tourism).

- Other interested groups—such as the state chambers of commerce; private sector security companies and stakeholders in providing rapid and mass transit; resident groups located in immediate proximity to stadiums; and the research and development (R&D) community involved with the public-private security collaboration.

This is not an exhaustive list of parties who might be interested in the contents of this thesis but provides an overview of the myriad of stakeholders who may benefit from an analysis of SEAR 4–5 event venue security.

E. THESIS OVERVIEW

Chapter II: Literature Review

The goal of this chapter is to identify what is known regarding current special event sporting venue security and what aspects or issues are not sufficiently addressed or researched to date. The review is organized into six sections, each of which will be explored in greater detail in Chapter II:

- Sporting event security threats
- Current doctrinal organization
- U.K. and E.U. approaches to sporting event security
- Technology in sporting venue security
- Legal review
- Cost benefit considerations

Reviewing the literature will yield a baseline understanding for an assessment of sporting event venue security and establish the framework for the analysis of the thesis. Any gaps identified in the overall picture of event venue security will then be researched using quantitative and/or qualitative methods for analysis in Chapter III.

Chapter III: Analysis and Findings

The intent of this chapter is to respond to the three research questions. Based on Chapter II's revelation of doctrinal weaknesses and possible organizational and technology employment strengths, this chapter will then examine the collection of data and information for quantitative and/or qualitative analysis. Chapter III will examine developing national and global trends in terrorism, sporting event exposure, and mega-event security. The trends will be analyzed with literature and data to weigh the concept of a growing viable threat of attack, or multiple coordinated attacks, against SEAR 4–5 rated sporting events. The second goal is to identify whether a cost-benefit relationship can be established to merit enhanced protective equipment or doctrinal measures that incur modest expense at SEAR 4–5 events. The final goal is to identify and introduce potential public policy roles, both those that bear little or no cost, and those that may bear significant government expense. However, the findings of the chapter will yield innovative funding streams to minimize the government expense to field long-term solutions.

Chapter IV: Summary

This chapter will revisit this thesis' problem statement and research questions to encapsulate how the research served to answer the questions. Conclusions drawn from Chapter III will be presented as recommendations toward innovative future security models. To move forward, a working group structure and purpose will be outlined. Thus, the end-state of this thesis will produce risk-reducing, cost-effective recommendations. These recommendations will serve the HSE by improving SEAR 4–5 event venue security in order to thwart another foreseeable catastrophic terrorist attack.

II. LITERATURE REVIEW

Political actors throughout history ... [have been] regularly trying to win over the masses and gain popular support by taking advantage of mass movements and profit from mass gatherings.

—Nobel Prize-winning novelist Elias Canetti

A. SPORTING EVENT SECURITY THREATS

In this chapter, the literature will be reviewed to facilitate better understanding of the nature and extent of the terrorist threat issues facing sporting event security teams.

One widely acknowledged definition of terrorism established by the United Nations articulates that targets are selected to maximize negative psychological effects on societies or governments.[30] To achieve this, and because of the nature of the power imbalance between terrorists and their sovereign government enemies, unorthodox or unanticipated selections of targets and delivery methods support the purpose to achieve utmost impact with the minimum resources available.[31] There is sufficient baseline literature to establish that terrorism is a successful strategy and is not likely to disappear from the tactical options available to outmanned, outgunned terrorist groups anytime soon.[32]

There is little question that the various terror cells around the world retain members that are fervently committed.[33] Because of the depth of devotion to their cause, members of groups and radicalized individuals can readily adapt to counterterrorism strategies

---

[30] Toohey, "Terrorism," 433.

[31] Fathali M. Moghaddam, *From the Terrorists' Point of View: What They Experience and Why They Come to Destroy* (Westport, CT: Greenwood, 2006), 5–6, 2006, citing, "Al Qaeda-inspired terrorist attacks have been designed to achieve maximum impact using minimum resources—the biggest 'bang for the buck.' "

[32] Kathryn Fisher, "From 20th Century Troubles to 21st Century International Terrorism: Identity, Securitization, and British Counterterrorism from 1968 to 2011," (Ph.D dissertation, The London School of Economics and Political Science, 2012).

[33] Moghaddam, *From the Terrorists' Point,* 4; David W. Brannan, and N.T. Anders Strindberg, *Critical Analysis of Terrorism and Terrorist Groups: A Handbook for Practitioners* (unpublished manuscript) 2013, 30.

meant to defeat them. The result is that terrorists will continually seek innovation in their technologies, delivery means, and targets.[34]

The literature reflects that often, if not routinely, terrorists are not madmen deranged by evil, but rather they are driven individuals reverting to rational, problem-solving strategies (in their view) to serve and promote their cause.[35]

The Defense Threat Reduction Agency found that professional subject matter experts in the intelligence community agreed that "terrorist [attack] innovation is usually motivated by problem solving intended to overcome constraints in the security environment, or limitations in the political one."[36] Furthermore, terrorists seek "new technologies, targets, or opportunities in order to circumvent security measures, revitalize support for their cause, pursue a new strategy to remedy failed ones, or simply to escalate a conflict because lower levels of violence are assessed to be ineffective."[37] These adaptations are classified as strategic, tactical, or organizational innovations in terrorism.[38]

To clarify between the first two of these adaptations, strategic innovation involves the development of new objectives for the terrorist organization.[39] It encompasses significant shifts in how groups frame their goals, and thus may require new forms of violence, target sets, or audiences to influence.[40] An example of strategic innovation was Al-Qaeda's shift from aiding insurgencies against "near enemies" (secular regimes in the Muslim world) to attacking the "far enemy" (Western countries).[41] Author Martha

---

[34] Mohammed Hafez and Maria Rasmussen, *Terrorist Innovations in Weapons of Mass Effect, Phase II. PASCC Report Number 2012 003* (Monterey, CA: Naval Postgraduate School, Center on Contemporary Conflict, January 2012), 4–5

[35] Moghaddam, *From the Terrorists' Point*, 5.

[36] Hafez and Rasmussen, *Terrorist Innovations in Weapons,* 4–5, citing Martha Crenshaw, "Innovation: Decision Points in the Trajectory of Terrorism," paper presented at the conference Trajectories of Terrorist Violence in Europe, Harvard University, Cambridge, Massachusetts, March 9–11, 2001.

[37] Ibid., 4–5

[38] Ibid., 39

[39] Ibid., 4–5

[40] Ibid., 39

[41] Ibid.

Crenshaw lists several other cases of strategic innovation: the Irgun's campaign against British authorities in Mandate Palestine in the 1940s; airline hijackings in the 1960s; Hezbollah's campaign of suicide bombings in the 1980s; and Aum Shinrikyo's sarin attack in 1995.[42]

On the other hand, tactical innovation involves significant shifts in technologies and techniques of terrorism without a concomitant change in objectives.[43] Consequently, Crenshaw avers that changes in weapons or targets occur more frequently in the life of terrorist organizations than does a fundamental strategic shift.[44] Among the examples she offers are the murder of Count Folke Bernadotte in 1948, which was the first time an international mediator was murdered, and the IRA's switch from attacking Ireland to attacking the British mainland.

The final form of innovation, organizational, is worth noting because of its application to global communications of the 21st century. Organizational innovation contains new ways of structuring the terrorist group or inventive methods to reach new recruits.[45] As cited in Chapter I, *Inspire* magazine has proven to be one such source used to cultivate and train homegrown radicals in America.

These three types of innovations are catalysts for the need for DHS to plan for the eventuality of the employment of new forms of attack by terrorists. The fact that certain targets have not yet been attacked does not preclude these targets from future attacks if they meet the goals and level of susceptibility deemed suitable by the terrorist. Tactically, innovative choices in target selections, timing of attack, and delivery method greatly exacerbate the challenge to the HSE. The challenges are more formidable when coupled with the practically oriented, demonstrated resolve to attack non-combatants and soft targets.

---

[42] Martha Crenshaw, "Innovation: Decision Points in the Trajectory of Terrorism," paper presented at the Conference on Trajectories of Terrorist Violence in Europe, Harvard University, Cambridge, MA, March 9–11, 2001.

[43] Hafez and Rasmussen, *Terrorist Innovations*, 39.

[44] Hafez and Rasmussen, *Terrorist Innovations*, citing Crenshaw, 5–6

[45] Ibid., 40

As Fathali Moghaddam points out, this, along with the perceived severity of the threat terrorists believe they face from the West (and most often, the U.S.), allows them to justify the attack of virtually anyone, anytime, anywhere.[46] Moghaddam further explains that from the terrorists' point of view, the acts they perpetrate against non-combatant civilians are part of a "rational problem-solving strategy."[47] Terrorists do not view themselves as "terrorists," they see themselves as warriors, freedom-fighters, or revolutionaries.[48] They envisage themselves as soldiers for a cause, "Commandos … attacking the United States and its forces at home and abroad in a declared world war."[49] Moghaddam expounds that although innocent civilians (as victims of the attacks) do not consider themselves as enemy combatants, the mindset of the attackers is unaltered, and they believe they are fully justified in conducting these attacks.

Notwithstanding the presumption that they may be able to strike in any nation, terrorists also understand that if they attempt to attack U.S. military forces in a conventional battle, they will be risking "organizational suicide."[50] Therefore, they embrace the rationale of attacking the civilian electorate to influence American leadership and foreign policy because it is the electorate who put the leaders into office.[51] It is the non-combatant citizens that share responsibility with leaders for attacks against the in-group terrorist organizations and Muslim nation-states.[52] The result is that unsuspecting civilians and soft targets are easy to strike. On occasion, as with the Madrid train bombings in 2004, such attacks can pay major dividends to the terrorist cause by virtue of swaying public opinion and, thereby, government action.[53]

In addition to the presence of media members and a sporting event's public visibility to the electorate and its government, several other key attributes render these

---

[46] Moghaddam, *From the Terrorists' Point*, 4–5

[47] Ibid., 2

[48] Brannan and Strindberg, "Critical Analysis of Terrorism," 30.

[49] Moghaddam, *From the Terrorists' Point*, 2.

[50] Ibid., 5

[51] Ibid.

[52] Ibid.

[53] Ibid.

events as desirable terrorist targets. Kristine Toohey asserts that "the terrorist power of uncertainty is potent because we live in a risk society, characterized by the cultural desire to control chance, be secure, and by institutions increasingly organized around risk management."[54] One advantage for terrorists against the stronger, organized society they attack lies in the unpredictability of the strike, hitting at places and times when non-combatants (victims) consider themselves safe.

This is one of the central features of the impact of terrorism, to strike when the society as target thinks that it is secure.[55] Richard Ericson and Aaron Doyle assess that the "fear culture" is present in western society now because terrorists promote the idea of uncertainty in society. This leads governments to focus more attention on security and certainty, which then continues the cycle for terrorists to find new ways to attack the vulnerability gap and promote the concept of uncertainty and fear.[56]

An additional aspect of modern terrorism strategy and tactics meriting review in this thesis is the rapid 21st century innovations in communications and cultural globalization, which are making it easier for terrorist groups to recruit, train, and deploy "lone wolf" and radicalized home-grown attackers.[57]

Department of Homeland Security Acting Secretary Randy Beer asserts:

> Lone offenders—prime targets of al-Qa'ida's English-language messaging, such as the online magazine *Inspire*—tend to favor plots involving the use of easily acquired weapons against local targets. These lone offender plots are especially challenging because they can be tactically simple and adaptable, complicating disruption by authorities.[58]

---

54 Toohey, "Terrorism," 432.

55 Ibid.

56 Richard Ericson and Aaron Doyle, *Uncertain Business: Risk, Insurance and the Limits of Knowledge* (Toronto: University of Toronto Press, 2004), 141.

57 Catarina Kinnvall, "Globalization and Religious Nationalism: Self, Identity, and the Search for Ontological Security." *Political Psychology* 25, no. 5 (2004): 741–767; Toohey, "Terrorism," 432.

58 *Threats to the Homeland: Hearing before the Senate Committee on Homeland Security and Government Affairs*, 112 Cong (2013) (statement of Rand Beers, Acting Secretary, Department of Homeland Security).

Further demonstrating the diverse origins of terrorists and the difficulty to identify and track them, a study of Islamic radicalization found that between 1989 and 2011, 211 individuals had radicalized in North America to the point of supporting violence.[59] Many of these individuals (80 percent) initiated their radicalization after the events of September 11, 2001.[60]

The innovations in their means and targets of attack are not, per se, new strategy, but like many terrorist organizations through the centuries, these latest innovations of how and where to attack are "unorthodox for their day."[61] For terrorists, impact, symbolism, and dramatic effect are all essential ingredients to successful attack.[62] Historically, terrorists have considered attacks upon larger stages as better platforms to promote their cause, while asserting their power over the host nation's inability to protect their people.[63]

Regarding the link between sports and terrorism, a watershed moment in history took place during the Munich Olympic Games in 1972. Some have even attributed this attack as ***THE*** defining moment in the growth of modern terrorism.[64] The worldwide broadcast of the video image of the terrorists at the 1972 Munich Olympics operation became the iconic symbol of 20th century international terrorism and was a source of inspiration for future attacks on the summer games.[65] Just the word "Munich" also became synonymous with the threat from extremely well-funded, nationalist, and religious-based terrorists such as the Palestine Liberation Organization (PLO).[66]

---

[59]National Consortium for the Study of Terrorism and Responses to Terrorism (START), *Fact Sheet: Violent Extremism in the U.S (*College Park, MD: START, December 9, 2011).

[60] Ibid.

[61] Fisher, "From 20th Century Troubles," 50.

[62] Toohey, "Terrorism," 432.

[63] Moghaddam, *From the Terrorists' Point*, 5–6

[64] Toohey, "Terrorism," 434.

[65] Hafez and Rasmussen, *Terrorist Innovations*, 9.

[66] Ibid., 2–3.

The PLO proclaimed a few weeks after the 1972 Summer Games that the propaganda of the Munich attack was an astounding 100 percent success. The attack's planner stated, "It was like painting the name of Palestine on a mountain that can be seen from the four corners of the Earth."[67] Because of the magnitude of the success of the Munich attacks, apparent to terrorists and counterterrorist experts alike, it was and still is reasonable to recognize that a moment such as that, occurring at a sporting venue, bestows some sense of importance to all sporting venues for generations to come.[68]

An additionally important HSE consideration arising out of the Munich attack was the manifestation of a "wild card" motivational factor. The Defense Threat Reduction Agency (DTRA) specifically cited the 1972 Munich Olympics as an example of practically driven strategic motivation. The PLO-backed Black September Organization executed the attack at the Games; however, the strategic impetus for the attack was directly linked to the expulsion of Palestinian guerilla factions from Jordan by the government. The PLO's defeat at the hands of the Jordanian government, combined with the loss of bases from which to attack Israel, greatly demoralized the PLO members and weakened their leaders.[69] Seeing the Olympics as a soft target sporting event (in that era), "The Munich operation was an attempt to regain legitimacy for the PLO's senior leaders after an ignominious defeat."[70] It is this element of inner organizational politics and strife prompting the organization to act at unanticipated times which serves as a strategic wild card factor.

With the literature setting the stage for the baseline terrorist threat faced by sporting event security teams, contemporary issues and data arising from the research found to be applicable to the thesis questions will be explored in the Analysis chapter later in this thesis. Qualitative issues of current doctrinal organization and standards of training, compliance, and inspections will be reviewed and addressed in greater detail in

---

67 Toohey, "Terrorism," 434.

68 Ibid.

69 Hafez and Rasmussen, *Terrorist Innovations*, 4–5

70 Ibid.

the Analysis chapter as well. However, to facilitate that qualitative analysis, the current doctrinal framework literature will be reviewed in the next section.

B.   CURRENT DOCTRINAL ORGANIZATION AND STRUCTURE

Complacency is the enemy of (homeland) safety.

> —British Lord Chief Justice Peter M. Taylor,
> *Final Report of Hillsborough Stadium Disaster*

In order to view the proper context of the current doctrine, known as the DHS National Planning Framework, it is important to briefly review the evolution from 2001 to the status quo reflected in the literature. This will facilitate a better understanding of past schools of strategic thought that were previously attempted or established. The intent of the later doctrinal analysis will be to reveal if there even is such a doctrine in place now, and if so, how effectively it is currently employed at sporting venues.

Following the al Qaeda attacks in 2001, the *9/11 Commission Report* revealed that the disparate security doctrine, equipment, and security methods practiced prior to 2001 contributed significantly to the failure of the security system dedicated to protecting the American public on that fateful day.[71] Subsequently, an underlying premise for the colossal increase of centralized government providing security was to synchronize multi-agency collaboration and the myriad state/local and private sector stakeholders through a single command and control institution.[72] Thereafter, the U.S. government experienced an Odyssean journey through the ensuing first decade's development of myriad documents, goals, strategies, tasks, and milestones in the name of homeland and national security.

Chronologically documenting the evolving nature of America's homeland and national security doctrine emanating from the 9/11 attacks in 2001, Sharon Caudle asserts that perceiving the criticality and immediacy of the terrorist threat to America, the federal government under the George W. Bush administration established terrorism as the

---

71 9/11 Commission, *The 9/11 Commission Report,* 4.

72 Aviation and Transportation Security Act of 2001, Pub L. No. 107–71, 114, 49 U.S.C. § 114 (2001).

primary domestic threat.[73] That led the president to claim in one early strategic planning document that terrorism was "a permanent national condition" and therefore homeland security as a new permanent fixture in federal government.[74] The direct result was the creation of the Department of Homeland Security, the issuance of a specific national homeland security strategy, and other major policy developments.[75]

Accordingly, over the subsequent years of the Bush administration, the federal government and newly founded DHS acknowledged the need to avoid stove-piped planning and envisioned the whole American community coming together as one entity to develop the complex preventive, protective, and responsive net to stop terrorism and be ready to recover from it .[76] The initial blueprint in the Presidential Office of Homeland Security's National Strategy (2002) and the President's Homeland Security Presidential Directive (HSPD-8, 2003) defined the whole community with the collaborative stakeholder relationships between federal, state, and local governments and non-governmental organizations along with the private sector. The Homeland Security Act of 2002 codified the central organizational point of leadership and policy development at the Department of Homeland Security (DHS).

In 2005, producing what it then deemed the "Interim National Preparedness Goal," DHS proclaimed it answered the questions, "How prepared do we need to be? How prepared are we [actually]?" and "How do we prioritize efforts to close the gap?"[77] In so doing, the Interim Goal identified 15 national planning scenarios and an extensive, comprehensive target capabilities list as two primary planning tools for use in the fledgling homeland security community. For example, the Interim Goal listed IEDs as one of the threat scenarios to prepare for and laid out a detailed description of how

---

[73] Sharon Caudle, "Homeland Security: Advancing the National Strategic Position." *Homeland Security Affairs* 8 (August 2012):2, http://www.hsaj.org/?article=8.1.11.

[74] Ibid.

[75] Ibid.

[76] Ibid., 3

[77] Ibid.

explosive trace detection equipment could be employed as a system of systems. The critical task list was then crafted to support the projected scheme.[78]

At this point, in 2005, the DHS and FEMA-based grants to the state/local governments were distributing much-needed support and had become prominent parts of fiscal year budgeting. There is no literature on whether the government had begun conceptualizing the various infrastructure sectors as separate lanes or industries that could be sought out to collaborate with and develop alternate forms of funding to meet these risk-based security needs.

In 2007, a new National Strategy for Homeland Security defined a full range of potentially catastrophic events including natural disasters, diseases, and man-made accidents. Also introduced was a Homeland Security Management System, intended to build on the operational and tactical level planning and activities detailed in the guidelines.[79] This served as a first example of a comprehensive system emplaced to provide evaluation and oversight inspection capabilities for planning and exercises or operations.

In summary of the first administration's view toward homeland security doctrine, it was established as a national community responsibility and not merely a federal government responsibility. It recognized the federal government control of policy strategy development "buttressed with federal grants to states and localities" to establish specific goals, performance targets, and measures. However, when the Obama administration took charge in early 2009, another shift in strategy took root and resulted in significantly altered goals and metrics.

In 2011, Presidential Policy Directive 8 (PPD-8) was released. PPD-8 decidedly marked the swing away from terrorism as a primary HSE focus to a posture built on flexibility and scalability to react to virtually any source of national or regional safety concern.[80] A significant change was to subsume Homeland Security doctrine under the

---

78 U.S. Department of Homeland Security (DHS), *Interim National Preparedness Goal, Homeland Security Presidential Directive 8: National Preparedness* (Washington, DC: DHS, March 31, 2005),.14

79 Caudle, "Homeland Security," 4.

80 Ibid., 5.

auspice of national security doctrine. The Obama administration assessed that there was a myriad of grave security issues meriting a broader security stance than just one focused on terrorism.[81] Also needing to be addressed with doctrine were social and political instability, health care issues, cyber threats, climate change, and weather hazards. The Obama administration also directed the HSE to begin preparing for simultaneous crises of varying kinds. This shift in viewpoint became relevant to sports venue security due to the seemingly more strategic level input role for the federal government (i.e., less specific about plans and task/compliance requirements than in the Bush administration era).

Introducing Core Capabilities to replace the formerly used 15 planning scenarios and accompanying target capabilities (task) list, the intent of the drastic reduction in specificity was to enable state/local authorities to tailor resource abilities with mission challenges in their respective regions.[82] Pursuant to PPD-8, DHS was required to produce National Planning Frameworks to address each of the homeland security mission areas.[83] The core capabilities were to be addressed in greater detail in each of the five mission areas' respective national planning framework document.

DHS released its *Overview of the National Planning Frameworks* in 2013. Rooted in the PPD, the overview consolidates summaries and key themes for the respective mission area frameworks. Further echoing the PPD, the overview also establishes that the initial conditions premising the respective frameworks are what the community and senior government leaders should do "upon the discovery of intelligence or information regarding an imminent threat to the homeland in order to thwart an initial or follow-on terrorist attack."[84] The overview defines that the respective frameworks are established in order to "explain and guide the Nation's approach for ensuring and enhancing national preparedness" in each respective mission area.[85] It further asserts they are intended to

---

[81]Caudle, "Homeland Security," 5–6.

[82] Ibid., 6–7

[83] U.S. Department of Homeland Security (DHS), Overview of the National Planning Frameworks (Washington, DC: DHS, May 1, 2013), 3

[84] Ibid.

[85] Ibid., 1

1. Set the strategy and doctrine for building, sustaining, and delivering the core capabilities identified in the National Preparedness Goal

2. Describe the coordinating structures and alignment of key roles and responsibilities for the whole community and integrate to ensure interoperability across all mission areas

3. Address the roles of individuals; nonprofit entities and nongovernmental organizations (NGOs); the private sector; communities; critical infrastructure; governments; and the Nation as a whole[86]

It acknowledges that the five respective mission areas represent "a spectrum of activity" and are "highly interdependent [with] ... regular coordination among departments and agencies working to prevent, protect against, mitigate, respond to, and recover from all threats and hazards."[87]

However, the overview presents planning frameworks for only four of the five mission areas. Conspicuously absent from the overview is the Protection Mission Framework. The overview also does not present any explanation as to why, as of May 2013, the framework is missing from the synthesized overview document. However, for analysis purposes, this thesis uses the still unapproved-for-release *Working Draft—National Protection Framework*,[88] which was originally circulated for input and approval in 2012.

The effectiveness of the Core Capabilities-based approach been called into question.[89] DHS has attempted to link dollars spent with the development of capabilities but without established metrics or a proven system of inspection, compliance verification, or evaluation. The Government Accountability Office (GAO) found that the Federal Emergency Management Agency (FEMA) lacked any standardization for data collection and overall data reliability yielding critical problems in its metrics and assessment process.[90] Therefore, there is room for alternative options to be raised that have already

---

86 DHS, *Overview*.

87 Ibid.

88 Federal Emergency Management Agency (FEMA), *Working Draft—National Protection Framework, Review Package, Presidential Policy Directive/PPD-8* (Washington, DC: FEMA, March 2012.

89 Caudle, "Homeland Security."

90 Ibid., 9.

been proven effective.[91]   Still to be resolved would be whether adoption of the management system preparedness standards should be mandated (perhaps tied to federal funding), and how certification or accreditation against the standards would be conducted. The question also remains whether such a compliance and evaluation system can be effectively implemented to ensure the building and sustaining of core capabilities if it is only voluntary.[92]

In conclusion, the literature reflects there is no national doctrine with specific equipment or procedural standards to be applied to sports venue security. Even with best practices offered for voluntary implementation, without effective compliance measures, the federal level has difficulty assuring the American people that the HSE is accomplishing the National Protection Mission. In the next section, the literature will be reviewed to examine how strategic doctrine is organized, inspected, and executed in the United Kingdom.[93]

C.   U.K. AND E.U. APPROACHES TO SPORTING EVENT SECURITY

Security professionals and U.S. government leaders must also recognize that constant threats of both organized and spontaneous terror have been managed with relative levels of success in ... Great Britain, which combats Catholic/Protestant aggression in addition to soccer hooligans, and ... [t]hough unfortunately acquired through horrid levels of sustained violence, certain elements from such international cognates of expertise may hold particular insight into security training for domestic venues in the United States.

—Benjamin D. Goss, Colby B. Jubenville, and Jon L. MacBeth,
*Primary Principles of Post-9/11 Stadium Security in the United States:
Transatlantic Implications from British Practices*

Venue managers, sporting league officials, security professionals and government officials on both sides of the ocean have cited their concerns of sporting venue terrorist

---

[91] Caudle, "Homeland Security," 9–10.

[92] Ibid., 10.

[93] Stacey A. Hall, "An Examination of British Sport Security Strategies, Legislation, and Risk Management Practices: Lessons Learned from the English Football League," *The Sport Journal* 13, no. 2 (2010): 1–7. http://www.thesportjournal.org/article/.

attack since 9/11.[94] José Luis Arnaut asserts that they are also concerned that terrorists may take a path of least resistance in carrying out attacks, seeking easily accessed targets with maximum disturbance potential and politically or economically symbolic value.[95] Goss, Jubenville, and MacBeth, note that though terrorists may desire to execute spectacular attacks, they are realistic in perceiving their own limited capabilities and therefore specifically seek softer targets of opportunity such as banks, shopping malls, places of recreation, and sports entertainment.[96] Further supporting that notion of smaller venue vulnerability Gary Lhotsky avers the concept that the larger the stadium and event, the better trained venue staff, crowd management and security practices. Attacking smaller events and venues offers the possibility of more mayhem and corollary damage or destruction.[97]

Whereas the U.S. National Protection Framework is still unpublished, and the federal government does not have an active presence at SEAR 4–5 events,[98] the United Kingdom effectively integrates national government doctrine with local law enforcement organizations to secure sporting venues.[99] Similarly, whereas the U.S. does not have a standard business practice that maximizes technology resources as part of venue security, the U.K. sets a global example in the use of technology at sporting events. The integration of the U.K. doctrine and its deployment of technology illustrate how the HSE can enhance and expand its ability to protect sports venues in the U.S.

The U.K. initiated a push on sporting event security in the 1980s, long before 9/11, as a response to "hooliganism." Gerald Griggs documents that this behavior of hooliganism started more than a century ago by some accounts, and may have originated

---

[94] Benjamin D. Goss, Colby B. Jubenville, and Jon L. MacBeth, *Transatlantic Implications from British Practices* (International Association of Assembly Managers, June 2003), 17–18.

[95] José Luis Arnaut, *Independent European Sport Review 2006* (UK Presidency of the EU 2005, October 2006).

[96] Goss, Jubenville, and MacBeth, *Transatlantic Implications*,17–18

[97] Gary Lhotsky, "An Analysis of Risk Management at NCAA Division I-A Football Stadiums, (Ph.D. diss. Florida State University, 2006).

[98] *Federal Support for and Involvement in State and Local Fusion Centers: Hearing before Permanent Subcommittee on Investigations, Committee on Homeland Security and Governmental Affairs*, 112th Cong., 2nd sess., October 3, 2012.

[99] Hall, "An Examination of British Sport Security Strategies."

out of enthusiasm toward supporting a sporting club and vehement opposition to an arch-rival club; however, it evolved into unbridled violence and crime casting a pall over the national pastime in England.[100] Over the course of the 1960s–1970s, such gangs as the Head Hunters from West London, the Inter City Firm from East London and the Bushwhackers from Millwall all became notoriously renowned for their routinely perpetrated criminal violence and mayhem.[101] By the 1980s, hooliganism had evolved into an extensive array of hoodlums throughout the nation which the U.K.'s law enforcement (LE) community found to be contributing toward corollary criminal activity. Drug trafficking, robbery, assault, kidnapping, and spontaneous violence summarily equated to terrorist behavior against the freedom and security of the British public.[102] In the 1990s, as technology advanced for CCTV, the IRA attack at Bishopsgate in Central London proved to be a catalyst for the expanded use of CCTV to provide security to public places.[103]

Meanwhile, the U.K. Parliament and Home Office considered hooliganism as evolving into a serious public threat and took proactive measures to use legislation, doctrine, and technology to prevent and combat it as it would for any other form of terrorism.[104] What arose was the development of centralized organization and doctrine to be implemented from the national level downward to the local level targeted to support local policing in its campaign to combat hooliganism and protect public order. This aggressive operational approach was reinforced with technology to maximize efficiency of costs and available resources. In time, it was recognized that the campaign against

---

[100] Gerald Griggs, "Soccer Hooliganism in England Between the Wars," *The Sport Journal* 7, no. 3 (2004): 1–5. http://www.thesportjournal.org/article/soccer-hooliganism-england-between-wars; Goss, Jubenville, and MacBeth, *Transatlantic Implications*, 3, citing *Football Violence in Europe* by Marsh, James, Anne Fox, Kate Fox, Giovanni Carnibella, Joe McCann, and Peter Marsh.

[101] A. J. Haley, "British Soccer Superhooligans: Emergence and Establishment: 1982–2000," *The Sport Journal* 4, no. 3 (2001). http://web.archive.org/web/20070221100029/.

[102] Goss, Jubenville, and MacBeth, *Transatlantic Implications*, 4, citing "Football Violence on the Rise," *BBC News*, August 15, 2001, hi/uk_news/1491743.stm.

[103] Michael McCahill and Clive Norris, *CCTV Systems in London. Their Structure and Practices*, Working Paper No.10 (Hull, UK: Centre for Criminology and Criminal Justice, University of Hull, April 2003), 2. http://www.urbaneye.net/results/.

[104] Ibid.

hooliganism was an effective model for defending venue locations and combating organized terror attacks at public venues.[105]

Though the U.S. sports market does not suffer from hooliganism to the extent that the U.K. had in the past, the doctrinal lessons learned and technology systems employed in combating hooliganism are applicable for HSE counterterrorism operations and sports venue security.

Another component of the U.K.'s success was due to the safety legislation which was passed requiring stadiums and club (private sector) ownership groups to acquire and maintain a "Safety Certificate." This was in accordance with the government's "set of safety requirements in the 'Guide to Safety at Sports Grounds' for every soccer team playing in the top four divisions in England."[106] The local governments issue the certificate and monitor event/stadium compliance with the requirements. Local LE also assigns a designated Safety Officer to assist facility management with safety strategies on match day.[107] The U.K. also developed an organizational Code of Practice and doctrine that originated at the national government level and disseminated down to the local law enforcement and event venue management level. The U.K.'s organization has no exact comparison in the U.S.

The U.K.'s national synchronization of sporting security effort begins with the United Kingdom Football Policing Unit (UKFPU), established in 2005, and accountable to the Home Office and the Association of Chief Police Officers (ACPO). The UKFPU is the UK's point of contact for collaboration with international counterparts, i.e., football policing "information points" designated, and it receives assistance from the U.K.'s National Counter Terrorism Security Office (NaCTSO).[108] The NaCTSO provides security in what the U.K. defines as "crowded places" (i.e., many public venues including shopping malls, mass transit stations, and sports venues). The ACPO has defined roles

---

[105] Goss, Jubenville, and MacBeth, *Transatlantic Implications,* 4.

[106] Hall, "An Examination of British Sport Security Strategies."

[107] Ibid.

[108] Association of Chief Police Officers (ACPO), *Guidance on Policing Football* (London: National Policing Improvement Agency, 2010), 54. http://www.acpo.police.uk/documents/uniformed/2010/201008UNGPF01.pdf.

and responsibilities for consistent application to local LE. These roles include each local police station whose area of responsibility envelopes a football stadium and various football clubs to have a football liaison officer (FLO), football intelligence officer (FIO), and police football spotters.[109] The UKFPU provides leadership, training, and guidance to FIOs, including the sharing and dissemination of threat intelligence updates.[110]

The FIO develops offender profiles and provides analytical assessments of events and participants, both as after action in review for learning purposes and in preparation for upcoming events.[111] One FIO intelligence product is a breakdown of event attendees into risk and non-risk attendees based on advance notice of ticket sales and identification of ticket purchasers.[112] Such a breakdown is essentially the application of a risk-based strategy to sporting events security.

The ACPO has also produced guidance for renovations and the new construction of stadiums in order to comply with safety legislation. In the initial conception of how to defend a site from an attack, the U.K. applies a logical approach to look at the site (venue) location itself, the structure, surrounding areas, gathering space in and outside of the venue. It then analyzes general access to the site in conjunction with the capabilities of an enemy (whether hooligan or terrorist) that is seeking that access.

Also becoming actively involved in the analysis and development of future venue security doctrine, the European Union (E.U.) has recognized that the World Cup tournament and others, like the UEFA Champions League matches, that are played throughout Europe and watched the world over, make for unprecedented platforms for international publicity. Because these events are suitable for various activities intended to attract public attention, such as demonstrations and peaceful protests, the E.U. recognized that "the modern constitutional democratic state needs to reconcile the risk of [terrorist

---

[109]ACPO, *Guidance on Policing*, 15.

[110] Ibid., 17.

[111] Ibid., 18.

[112] Ibid., 10.

attack] ... with the degree of surveillance and other preventive law enforcement procedures."[113]

Accordingly, a working group of professionals and scholars was commissioned to assess future protection mission possibilities and to begin constructing a path of milestones to achieve it. The consortium, *Supporting Fundamental Rights, Privacy and Ethics in Surveillance Technologies* (SAPIENT), recognized the impact of the 1994 and 2010 attacks at World Cup gathering sites in Djibouti, Ulster, and Somalia. These attacks, yielding 87 killed and 97 wounded, revealed the vulnerability of the communities surrounding venues and linked to sporting events, rendering them necessary to be included in security plans. SAPIENT is working for the long-term toward the security model of the next decade built upon three pillars:

- The preventive and precautionary collection, storage and processing of vast amounts of data on football fans, tourists and local citizens being considered actively or passively involved in the World Cup
- Surveillance in and around the stadiums of people and objects
- Monitoring of places with relevance to the World Cup events and venues such as lodging areas for the national teams, public viewing areas of fans and transportation hubs[114]

The SAPIENT projection is a visionary, but feasible doctrine blended with the best surveillance and detection technology resources either available now or in proto-type for the not too distant future.

---

[113] Philip Schütz et al., S*mart Surveillance and Securing Public Spaces*. SAPIENT Report # 261698 (Germany: Fraunhofer ISI, 2012), 2, https://www.hsdl.org/?view&did=734129.

[114] Schütz et al., S*mart Surveillance,* 3

D.   TECHNOLOGY IN SPORTING VENUE SECURITY

A security system is a combination of multiple components that must work together seamlessly to provide the appropriate level of protection for a facility.

—*DHS Reference Manual to Mitigate Potential Terrorist Attacks against Building*

Security Operations Centers (SOC or control centers) have sprung up at many major sporting facilities throughout America [Anderson 2010].[115]   At the SOC, security management teams receive input from various intelligence resources such as state fusion centers, human intelligence, and on-site venue technology resources. The SOC routinely will also have numerous video monitors linked to CCTV systems covering the vast acreage of a sports complex coupled with the ability to communicate immediately with security forces on the ground at the facility as well as with local community first responders. It is at the SOC that security management teams can leverage and monitor available technological resources.[116]

This section reviews the available technology resources which support facility protection and counterterrorism plans. The four primary forms of technology support to venue security operations that will be addressed in this thesis are Closed-Circuit Television (CCTV), X-ray screening systems, metal detectors, and Explosive Trace Detection (ETD).[117]

Since 9/11, DOD and DHS/HSE have invested vast amounts of time and funding into numerous forms of technology research and development (R&D) for security equipment technology, and there has been a heavy emphasis on ETD.[118]   ETD

---

[115] Teresa Anderson, "How Dallas Does Security" *Security Management*, 2010, http://www.securitymanagement.com/article/how-dallas-does-security-007656

[116] U.S. Department of Homeland Security (DHS), *Reference Manual to Mitigate Potential Terrorist Attacks against Buildings*, 2nd ed., FEMA-426/BIPS-06 (Washington, DC: DHS, October 2011), 5–10

[117] DHS, *Reference Manual*, 5–9. Security equipment also includes screening and contraband detection devices, such as, security XC-ray (e.g., explosive, weapons, backscatter), trace type detection (e.g., explosive, chemical, radiological), and magnetometers (metal detection).

[118] "MIT Lincoln Laboratory Wins Two R&D 100 Awards," Lincoln Laboratory, July 2013, http://www.ll.mit.edu/news/2013-RnD100awards.html; "Detecting Explosives Remotely," *R&D Magazine*,

technology capabilities include the inspection of people, containers, and objects. This technology bears intrinsic value for counterterrorism protective measures.[119]

In 2004, members of Sandia National Laboratories published the *Survey of Commercially Available Explosives Detection Technologies and Equipment, 2004.*[120] Although now dated, this document provides an excellent foundational analysis of various technologies still available to detect trace and bulk explosives and presents system characteristics that should be considered before investing in one type of ETD technology over another. From 2001–2007, R&D focused on sensors operating on different transduction principles, ranging from electrochemical to immune-sensors electrochemical sensors. For the ensuing five-year period through 2012, optical or laser-based technology had largely become the primary focus of R&D.

However, throughout the period, numerous stubborn technical challenges arose to continually thwart the intent of developing an accurate system that could detect explosives at a beneficial stand-off range to security operations. To sum up the major challenges, a trace detector would essentially seek a particulate matter in the air that exhibited molecular structures identical to the chemical element inherent in the combustible material. But because many different objects may contain natural elements which are also present in man-made explosives, ETD inaccuracy and high false alarm rates greatly diminish the value of the system.

Further complicating the detection effort, people may be exposed to objects which contain such elements and therefore not only certain objects can cause false alarms, but people can as well. Other factors that would diminish accuracy and stand-off ability to find trace elements included sunlight, wind, rain, and objects consisting of combinations

---

August 29, 2013, http://www.rdmag.com/award-winners/2013/08/detecting-explosives-remotely, citing PHASE team members Robert Haupt, Rosalie Bucci, Jae Kyung, Leaf Jiang, Charles Wynn, Napoleon Thantu, and Francesca Lettang.

[119] Malcolm McLellan III, "Tailoring Screening Technology to Prevent or Deter Terrorists from Attacking Commercial Ferries with Improvised Explosive Devices" (Master's thesis, Naval Postgraduate School, 2010), 11.

[120] Lisa Thiesen et al., "Survey of Commercially Available Explosives Detection Technologies and Equipment," (Albuquerque, NM: Sandia National Laboratories, 2004).

of chemical elements.[121] Therefore, if the ETD system could be positioned close enough to objects or people, and especially if in a somewhat controlled environment, then it could achieve tremendous accuracy. This is how the systems are now deployed at airports across the country.[122]

As of 2013, the industry best practices implemented meant explosives screening was conducted manually, visually, by swabbing, and through X-ray inspections.[123] Because these systems all involved being in the same virtual proximity, or in contact with, the person or container/object to be screened, they cannot be used in any sort of covert facility protection operation. These non-covert approaches can also be time-consuming because they are not able to screen crowds or large expanses of space, e.g., when throughput of a large crowd is required as at a sporting event.[124] Therefore, ETD systems have been of limited use for advance warning or interdicting against a "terrorist smart bomb" (i.e., an explosive-vest wearing suicide attacker).[125]

However, in late 2013, possibly a major breakthrough in technology was announced which rekindled the realistic possibility of ETD technology for deployment at sporting venues. The "cutting edge" discovery is the science of Photoacoustic Sensing of Explosives (PHASE).[126] This technology works with a combination of laser and audio technology. In summary, a laser pulse is sent out from a device, and when it strikes an object or person, it will "excite" elements on or in the subject of the scanning. The exciting of the element means to cause the element to emit an infinitesimal vapor. This process is similar to already established ETD systems; however, the new technology discovered is that in emitting the vapor, explosive elements actually release a form of

---

[121] Ibid.

[122] Transportation Security Administration (TSA), "Recommended Security Guidelines for Airport Planning, Design and Construction," May 2011, 96

[123] Robert Haupt, "Photo-acoustic Sensing of Explosives," *Tech Notes*, November 2013, http://www.ll.mit.edu/publications/technotes/TechNote_PHASE.pdf

[124] McLellan, "Tailoring Screening Technology," 10.

[125] Bruce Hoffman, "Defending America Against Suicide Terrorism," in *Three Years After, Next Steps in the War on Terror* (2005), 21–22; Moghaddam, *From the Terrorists' Point*, 3

[126] Haupt, "Photoacoustic Sensing of Explosives."

unique "audio" signal, or vibration wave. The unique "audio" signal, virtually unaffected by environmental elements, is detectable by laser vibrometry up to 100m away.

The accuracy of the tests, to date, have met with professional standards, exhibiting a superior accuracy of subject location designation to within millimeters, and a significantly lower false alarm rate when compared to heritage technologies.[127] Furthermore, the photo-acoustic system is also much more compact than the other technologies. It requires significantly less power to execute, permitting it to be deployed covertly and adding another dimensionality of deterrence to site venue protection.[128] In addition to ETD systems potentially aiding sports venue protection, CCTV has also become an integral part of effective security operations.

CCTV systems have been a part of the English sporting event system layered approach to technology for decades.[129] Since the 2001 attacks, CCTV usage has increased dramatically in the U.S. as well. Today's sporting and concert (cultural) event stadiums and arenas (venues) often cost hundreds of millions of dollars to build, with some even topping the $1 billion mark.[130] In the 21st century, construction of these modern venues presents opportunities for the most current security technologies and architecture to be built-in. One of this era's newest venue marvels, Texas Stadium, is complete with more than 260 Closed Circuit (CC) TV cameras.[131]

There are too many types and choices of cameras suited for many different environments and purposes to effectively review and address them all in this thesis. However, with regard to sports venue security, this thesis will categorize them into two general groups: low resolution and high resolution. Lower resolution CCTVs can be

---

[127] Ibid.

[128] Ibid.

[129] Hall, "An Examination of British Sport Security Strategies."

[130] Jeff Mosier, "The Cost of Cowboys Stadium Has Escalated to $1.2 billion," *Dallas Morning News*, April 1, 2010, http://stadiumblog.dallasnews.com/2010/04/the-cost-of-cowboys-stadium-ha.html

[131] Anderson, "How Dallas Does Security." "There are 263 CCTV cameras, both analog and digital, and more than 600 access control points. The camera feeds are recorded and also monitored live from an on-site control room (A second on-site control room is used solely to monitor traffic conditions around the stadium.) The primary control room is staffed by security officers as well as two officers from the Arlington Police Department who monitor texts and emails from fans."

effectively used for their wide-sweeping viewing capability to cover large swaths of space. This brings an added dimension of security team personnel efficiency. Cameras put "eyes on" locations and "patrol" multiple areas without expending human resources by employing numerous officers on the beat to cover the same logistical area. Beneficially, once identifying incidents as they occur, the SOC can either coordinate an effective and appropriate response or choose to conserve manpower by determining that no response is necessary.[132]   Additionally, lower resolution cameras are routinely less expensive and can be installed to provide a sweeping view of a scene in order to detect actions as they occur or subject behaviors indicating imminent events about to happen.[133]

High resolution cameras, on the other hand, are capable of quickly ascertaining fine details within a scene, and are therefore excellent resources to locate and identify potential threat individuals.[134]   Facial recognition is a developing technology and identifies faces in camera view and compares them against a known database.[135]   An optimal image is captured with at least moderate lighting and users facing toward a camera.[136]   The stiffest challenge to their performance is to automatically identify a person without active cooperation or consistent and favorable conditions for a high-resolution camera (e.g., identifying individuals from within a large, moving crowd located outdoors).[137]   Therefore, in past years they may have been an expensive resource misused on a subway platform, a parking lot, or a pedestrian avenue of approach to a sporting venue.[138]

---

[132] U.S. Department of Justice (DOJ), Office of Justice Programs (OJP), "CCTV: Constant Cameras Track Violators," *National Institute of Justice (NIJ) Journal*, no. 249 (July 2003): 16–23.

[133] U.S Department of Homeland Security (DHS), *Defining Video Quality Requirements: A Guide for Public Safety*, (Washington, DC: DHS, May 2013), 13–18

[134] Harry Wechsler, *Reliable Face Recognition Methods* (New York: Springer: 2007), 123–125

[135] Edmund Spinella, *Biometric Scanning Technologies: Finger, Facial and Retinal Scanning* (Bethesda, MD: SANS Institute, May 28, 2003), http://www.sans.org/reading_room/whitepapers/authentication/biometric-scanning-technologies-finger-facial-retinal-scanning

[136] Ibid.

[137] Wechsler, *Reliable Face Recognition,* 123–125

[138] DHS, *Defining Video Quality,* 13–18.

However, CCTV is rapidly becoming more effectively employed in a crowd to locate particular mannerisms. One such trait is gait, the identification of which may be predictive of an individual in a crowd walking with a heavily weighted object concealed within his or her clothing, such as a bomb vest.[139] Cameras with a shorter lens and greater aperture are capable of providing a wider spectrum of view and are more competent to transmit effective imagery while in various, or darker, lighting conditions.[140] These cameras may also be equipped with some smart capability to better identify individuals with suspicious behavior, such as subjects in view standing, loitering in one place to the SOC.[141] Providing a real-time feed to a SOC on-site, it can then be possible to deploy security teams more efficiently to evaluate or interdict in a scenario, often as far from the target venue as possible. Much like the potential benefit provided by accurate ETD, effective CCTV usage can provide the best stand-off range, i.e., protective buffer time and space from the attacker's high payoff target location.

Facial recognition is a CCTV benefit that is continually improving. There exist numerous variations of mathematical formulas and means (e.g., using decision trees, to take the machine's captured image and translate that through a comparison process into actionable intelligence).[142] FaceTrac is one system that has become a leader in the field. FaceTrac captures faces from the video stream and compares them with images stored in a database. Once a subject has been identified, FaceTrac notifies security personnel with a user-configured prompt or alert, greatly increasing the effective operational use of existing security manpower on location.

Proponents of employing facial recognition systems also cite that these systems require less concentration from human staff to monitor the video, making security operations more efficient by freeing some employees for other tasks.[143] Thereby smaller venue security teams can cover larger areas while simultaneously facial recognition

---

[139] "If Looks Could Kill," *The Economist*, October 23, 2008, ww.economist.com/node/12465303, citing Frank Morelli from Aberdeen Proving Ground.

[140] DHS, *Defining Video Quality*, 13–18.

[141] "If Looks Could Kill," *The Economist*.

[142] Wechsler, *Reliable Face Recognition*, 123–125

[143] Ibid., 21.

systems can lead to a greater number of officers on patrol or in being accurately guided in on where to go to make arrests.[144]

However, there is a lack of available literature that thoroughly addresses the operational and legal risks created by the utilization of facial recognition CCTV. Questions that require solutions include which databases to use, what training procedures are used for on-site security staff, and what is the potential liability deriving from false-positive alarms at the venue? These solutions are as integral to fielding future doctrine as is the success of the science itself.

In the literature, there exists explicit descriptions of the technical aspects of CCTV. However, for the purpose of this thesis, the paramount importance of the literature review is that it reflects the steady technology improvements made to establish CCTV and facial recognition as viable components of the venue security model worthy of analysis in the next chapter.

Metal detectors and X-ray screening equipment have been in use for many years. Because metal detectors are effective but limited in the span of their use, this thesis will not address literature regarding future possibilities. What is of importance is that metal detectors can be counted on for future employment in venue security operations. Major League Baseball will be requiring all of its (SEAR 4) venues to install metal detectors as a doctrinal upgrade before the beginning of the 2015 season.[145]

Similarly worth noting, since 2008, Customs and Border Protection (CBP) has employed a low (dosage) level X-ray system known as "Z Portal" for use in inspecting automobiles at border crossings and checkpoints.[146]

---

[144] Ibid.

[145] Greg Johns, "Safeco Field Adding Metal Detectors for Added Security, *MLB.com*, January 21, 2014, http://mlb.mlb.com/news/article/mlb/fans-to-pass-through-metal-detectors-at-safeco-field-beginning-this-season?ymd=20140121&content_id=66900582&vkey=news_mlb.

[146] U.S. Customs and Border Protection (CBP). "Fact Sheet: Z-Portal Vehicle Imaging System." August 2008. http://www.cbp.gov/linkhandler/cgov/newsroom/fact_sheets/port_security /z_portal.ctt/z_portal.pdf.

Figure 1.   Z Portal X-Ray at CBP Canadian Border Checkpoint

The same manufacturer of the Z Portal, American Science and Engineering (ASE), also produces a mobile version of the portal that is mounted inside a van or truck.[147] Known as the ZB Van, this resource can be used to go through parking lots scanning for threat items concealed in vehicles.

Transitioning from what is currently available to what can be considered for future use, there are several creative scenarios worth recognition. The European Union's SAPIENT project demonstrates a vision of a detailed venue security team scenario synchronizing all four resources with real-time audio and video communications and security patrols on the ground.[148] Another possible future innovation for application at sporting venues is currently being developed in the aviation transportation industry. Since 2001, the International Air Transport Association (IATA) has evolved as a global organization with participation and support from more than 240 airlines and 19 international governments, including the U.S.[149] The "Checkpoint of the Future" (COF) is a model checkpoint system that is being tested in the field by IATA.[150]

---

[147] "ZBV," AS&E, accessed April 4, 2014, http://as-e.com/products-solutions/cargo-vehicle-inspection/mobile/product/zbv/.

[148] Philip Schütz et al., *Smart Surveillance,* 4.

[149] Peter Murray, "IATA Unveils Checkpoint of Future," Jun3 28, 2011, *Singularity HUB*, http://singularityhub.com/2011/06/28/iata-unveils-the-airport-checkpoint-of-the-future/; "Press Briefing by DHS Secretary Napolitano and IATA Director-General Bisignani," U.S. Mission Geneva, January 22, 2010. https://geneva.usmission.gov/2010/01/23/napolitano-bisignani/.

[150] James Shillinglaw, "IATA to Focus on Fast Travel, Checkpoint of the Future to Improve Air Travel," *TravelPulse*, October 16, 2012, www.travelpulse.com/iata-to-focus-on-fast-travel-checkpoint-of-the-future-to-improve-air-travel.html.

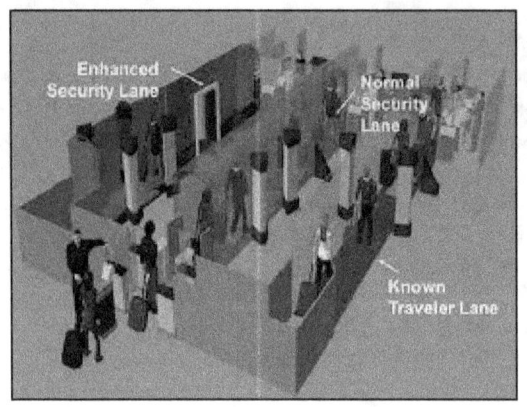

Figure 2.   IATA Models of the "Checkpoint of the Future" Prototype

As Figure 2 displays, a Checkpoint of the Future (COF) is modeled as a hallway or tunnel-type device that is intended for screened subjects to walk through without the need to stop and remove clothing or personal items. The intent of the global airline industry and security organizations is that the COF is improves the traveler experience by rendering the screening and inspection process as user-transparent to customers while vastly increasing throughput capacity, safely admitting people beyond the checkpoint with little reduction from the normal flow of movement.[151]

The IATA model uses advanced biometrics for identity confirmation[152] and draws from private sector (airline) and government collaboration to implement a risk-based screening (RBS) security model. This approach will identify passengers worthy of enhanced security screening apart from low-risk travelers, i.e., rather than the one-size-fits-all approach of looking for objects that may pose a threat or be used by a terrorist when onboard a plane.[153] This style of risk-based security may someday be applicable for sporting events, but that is a topic for future research and consideration in the HSE.

---

[151] A. Pawlowski, "Is This the Checkpoint of the Future?" *CNN.com*, June 7, 2011, http://articles.cnn.com/2011-06-07/travel/checkpoint.of.the.future_1_airport-checkpoint-airport-security-traveler-program?_s=PM:TRAVEL.

[152] Spinella, *Biometric Scanning Technologies*.

[153] Ibid.

The four primary forms of technology support reveal many benefits to security operations, but they also unveil several very relevant legal issues of concern in the HSE, which will be addressed in the next section.

E. LEGAL REVIEW

Whatever the after-the-fact analysis of the duty of care may be for a specific incident, the fundamental question will always be whether or not reasonable steps were taken to protect against an incident in light of the availability of security measures, the industry "standards" for security, and the potential threat of terrorism.

—Ronald E. Hurst, Catherine Pratsinakis, and Paul H. Zoubek,
"American Sports As A Target of Terrorism: The Duty of Care after
September 11th"

A review of the literature reveals that two primary legal issues of relevance exist related to sporting event venue security and counterterrorism operations: the duty of care (liability) and privacy.

Liability for patron and athlete participant safety rests with the owners, operators, supervisors, or possessors of land (venue manager) of sports venues.[154] Since 9/11, judicial trends regarding duty of care for security have leaned toward abrogation of government immunity, opening the opportunity for schools and universities to be sued.[155]

Therefore, private sector professional sporting event and collegiate athletic venue managers owe a duty of care to a patron attending the event. The legal term for the patrons' status is that of "invitee," and it is accorded the highest legal duty of obligation from the venue manager to provide for the safety of the patrons. The obligation to provide for the patrons' safety entails several primary aspects, but the one most relevant to sports venue managers is to conduct operations on the premises with reasonable care preventing the patrons from harm due to being hurt by others while there. This means that

---

[154] Ibid.

[155] Lhotsky, "An Analysis of Risk Management."

venue managers must take reasonable actions to protect patrons from "foreseeable" harm.[156]

If injured, wounded, or killed at a sporting event due to a terrorist attack, on reviewing the facts of a patron's case against a venue manager, one essential question to be answered by a court will be whether there existed a generally foreseeable risk to determine the existence of a duty and to limit the scope of the duty found. Stanford v. Kuwait Airways Corp., 89 F.3d 117, 125 (2d Cir. 1996) (airline had duty to protect passengers from risk of terrorists boarding connecting flight). The court of appeals in Stanford found that the hijacking of a plane was a generally foreseeable risk. The judicial rationale was that the airline-defendant's complacency had created a "zone of risk" and passengers would not have been harmed if the airline had reasonably mitigated the vulnerability beforehand.[157]

In this example, the court recognized that the airline had four sets of information that constituted it as having a general ability to foresee a terrorist attack:

> (1) threatened [airline attacks in general] by Hezbollah terrorists; (2) that terrorists were boarding flights in . . . airports to infiltrate other airlines; (3) that the Beirut airport had extraordinarily poor security; and (4) that the four hijackers who boarded in Beirut had tickets which teemed with suspicion. A jury could reasonably find, under these circumstances, that if [the airline] did nothing, it would create a zone of risk that stretched at least as far as the innocent passengers aboard flights with which the four hijackers would eventually connect.

In the past 13 years since the 9/11 terrorist attacks on New York and Washington, DC, the United States has had numerous instances of a heightened security alert status with various terrorist threats to American public safety. Though DHS retired the color-coded alert system in 2011 and has not enacted its replacement, the National Terrorism Advisory System does send alert bulletins to sectors and regions of the nation when various security risks arise.[158]

---

[156] Hurst, Pratsinakis, and Zoubek, "American Sports."

[157] Ibid.

[158] "National Terrorism Advisory System," U.S. Department of Homeland Security (DHS), accessed April 4, 2014, http://www.dhs.gov/national-terrorism-advisory-system.

As a result, terrorist attacks could very well be considered generally foreseeable, or "within the range of apprehension."[159] Customarily, the courts have found evidence of substantially similar prior criminal acts may be used to demonstrate that the landowner had actual or constructive knowledge of risk of harm to the invitee.[160] The term 'substantially similar' does not mean identical, but rather, whether the prior crimes committed elsewhere would have put a reasonable landowner on notice that visitors, residents, invitees, were subject to increased risk of harm. The question is whether the prior activity would have attracted the attention of a reasonably prudent landowner, and caused him to be concerned about the safety of the invitees.

What is required to be foreseeable is the general character of the event or harm, not the precise nature of the activity or the precise manner of its occurrence.[161] In particular, based on historical records linking sports to terrorism, venue operators and owners should be more aware of the risk that an American sporting event that attracts thousands of spectators could be a target of terrorist attack.[162] By failing to act or institute increased safety measures because of complacency or other reasons, venue owners and operators could be creating a zone of risk and be liable for a breach of the duty of care to invitees.[163]

Judicial precedent regards sporting events as a potential target of terrorism for the foreseeable future.[164] The scope of duty for venue managers, therefore, requires that reasonable measures be taken to protect against terrorist acts. Terrorist attacks may no longer be characterized as unforeseeable, creating a heightened duty of care owed by owners and operators to spectators, participants, and employees.[165]

---

[159] *Palsgraf v. Long Island R.R. Co.*, 162 N.E.2d 99.

[160] Robert D. Bickel, *Legal Issues Related To Silent Video Surveillance*. Washington, DC: The Security Industry Association and The Private Sector Liaison Committee, April 8, 1999, citing Shoney's Inc. v. Hudson, and Cohen v. Southland Corporation.

[161] Bickel, *Legal Issues Related To Silent Video Surveillance*.

[162] Hurst, Pratsinakis, and Zoubek, "American Sports."

[163] Ibid.

[164] Ibid.

[165] Ibid.

Lhotsky assesses that "in the 21st century, risk management will become a close companion to the sport business industry in its attempt to reduce losses and exposures, while increasing the desire to make the sport business industry safer."[166] This reveals that an incentive for private sector venue managers is that the reduction in vulnerability translates into corporate insurance savings.[167] There are numerous best practices that are suggested for venue managers to implement in order to constitute taking reasonable steps to reduce liability in protecting from terrorist attacks at their facilities. Hiring and vendor background checks, security operations doctrines, personnel training standards on the guidelines, and invoking exercises to drill and test incident response plans are all examples of venue managers taking effective measures to protect patrons from terrorism.[168]

The literature review reflects that privacy is also a relevant legal issue regarding the use of surveillance technologies at sporting events. However, whereas liability issues infer a duty on venue managers to stay current with equipment and security best practices to protect patrons, the privacy and civil liberties issue is more germane to the basic thresholds necessary to execute select security operations.

Citing "privacy rights" violations,[169] there have been and will likely continue to be objections to the use of CCTV, facial-scan technology, and other certain scanning and inspection techniques. Aside from the constitutional argument, there have been and will be opponents of the technology that will claim that its implementation and use is costly and ineffective in bringing about arrests, convictions, or real-time interdiction to prevent crime.[170] Additionally, opponents contend that its use furthers the negative image of

---

[166] Lhotsky, "An Analysis of Risk Management," 15.

[167] Keating, "Industry of Fear."

[168] Hurst, Pratsinakis, and Zoubek, "American Sports."

[169] Edmund Spinella, *Biometric Scanning Technologies*; see also self-proclaimed Civil Liberties watchdog group, The Young Turks, YouTube video, 5:51, October 1, 2010,http://www.youtube.com/watch?v=SZ2YW7-4Gbw.

[170] Bickel, *Legal Issues Related to Silent Video Surveillance.*

policing and security operations by fostering the "big brother is watching you" atmosphere.[171]

However, the longstanding "objectively reasonable expectation" test administered in courts today has consistently rendered a lowered expectation of privacy in automobiles than for a private residence.[172] That standard is lowered even further when a subject is in another's auto, or when going onto another's private property or onto municipal, state, and federal property.[173] Furthermore, the courts have consistently and specifically ruled that while in public view, there is no right to privacy from being watched on CCTV.[174]

Although the element of cost did arise in this section as an argument posed by opponents of CCTV surveillance, technology expense and the cost-benefit analysis theories found in literature will be addressed in the next, final section of the review.

F.   COST-BENEFIT ANALYSIS

Cost-benefit analyses are important because they help decision makers determine which protective measures, for instance, investments in technologies or in other security programs, will provide the greatest mitigation of risk for the resources that are available.

—John Mueller and Mark G. Stewart,
Terror, Security, and Money: Balancing the Risks, Benefits, and Costs of Homeland Security

In the era of austere fiscal climates there exist political strategic stances claiming either a diminished threat from terrorism, thereby questioning security expenditures, or alternatively, a focus on resilience after the fact of the rare attack which may occur. Similarly, there are sources in the reviewed literature that make the argument that many government expenditures for homeland security are not worthwhile. Before HSE senior

---

[171] Ibid.

[172] Katz v. United States, 389 U.S. 347, 88 S .(1976);

[173] Rakas v. Illinois, 439 U.S. 128, 99 S (1978)

[174] Bickel, *Legal Issues Related to Silent Video*, citing, L. R. Willson and Sons v. Occupational Safety & Health Review Commission, also, Secretary of Labor v. Concrete Construction Co.

leaders make vital decisions in how to allocate scarce resources, it is essential that proper attention and thorough cost-benefit analysis be weighed in consideration.

Crenshaw, Zulaika, and Burrows are among those that contend that the costs for DHS and the HSE are a waste of government funds that could be more effectively spent on socio-economic domestic policies. However, one of the foremost opponents of government spending in homeland security are Mueller and Stewart.

Mueller and Stewart offer multiple arguments for why the benefit does not outweigh the cost. He demonstrates quantitative data asserting that there is little viable terrorist threat targeting Americans,[175] and that the enemy specter portrayed to Americans is largely conjured as justification of the government, the media, and private sector stakeholders in the "terrorism industry." Further, it is the Mueller and Stewart formula that will be used to conduct the cost-benefit analysis later in this thesis to determine a breakeven point at which it is conducive to seriously consider enhanced security measures for the SEAR 4–5 softer targets.

However, these are not the only sources in the literature that explore costs of the HSE counterterrorism effort. Literature exists demonstrating that the costs to American society at the hands of a successful terrorist attack are as overwhelmingly staggering as the numbers presented in assessing its cost to combat it , the direct and indirect costs, and the short to long term economic impact.

Further, numerous sources affirm that terrorism will always be a threat to American society and that the question of the next successful, horrific attack within the U.S. is not if, but when. This means that the government will always need budget expenditures for homeland security to some degree. Governments abroad also recognize that terrorist organizations will adapt to survive, using new technology, new strategies, and may become capable of conducting more lethal operations.[176] Accordingly, the

---

[175] John Mueller and Mark G. Stewart, *Terror, Security, and Money: Balancing the Risks, Benefits, and Costs of Homeland Security* (Oxford, UK: Oxford University Press, 2011), 44

[176] United Kingdom Home Office, *The United Kingdom's Strategy for Countering International Terrorism*. Command Paper Number Cm 7547 (London: United Kingdom Home Office, March 24, 2009). https://www.hsdl.org/?view&did=32602

ideology associated with al Qaeda and groups like it will almost certainly adapt and outlive changes to their respective structure or group existence.[177]   Even among opponents of large expenditures on homeland security, there is concurrence that as long as there are animosities and hostilities among groups in the world, be they sovereign nation v. sub-nation organization, or just tribe versus tribe, terrorism has historically existed and always will.[178]

Regarding expenditures on sporting events, Olympic Games security and SEAR 1 events in America are all well documented, costing hundreds of millions of dollars.[179] The results are exemplary; since the 1972 Munich Games there have been no major terrorist attacks at the venues of the Games.[180] The literature also suggests that because of the success of the security at these mega-events, that terrorist attack plans have targeted related locations to attack instead. Locations outside of the venues at the Olympics and World Cup events, where patrons gather to view them, have been targeted since 1996.[181]

The damages and costs related to suffering a terrorist attack are many and will be addressed in detail in the Analysis chapter. However, the myriad cost factors highlighted in the literature lead to two questions to be resolved in this thesis:

1.   Is there a cost-benefit analysis that can be conducted to show that it is in the interest of either the private sector or public policy to invest in the cost of improving SEAR 4–5 security technologies and staff training; and

2.   Even if the cost might be exorbitant for a private sector sports league or team ownership group, might it be something that public policy can creatively venture into with the private sector to jointly support the cost to make upgrades work?

---

[177]United Kingdom Home Office, *The United Kingdom's Strategy.*

[178] Mueller and Stewart, *Terror, Security, and Money.*

[179] White House, Office of the Press Secretary, "Preparing for the World: Homeland Security and Winter Olympics," news release, January 10, 2012, https://www.hsdl.org/?view&did=475294; Rob King, "Olympics Run £2 Billion Over-Budget as Security Costs Double Due to Poor Planning," *Daily Mail*, March 9, 2012, http://www.dailymail.co.uk/news/article-2112489/London-2012-Olympics-runs-2bn-budget-security-costs-double.html.

[180] START, *Fact Sheet.*

[181] Ibid.

Both of these questions support the thesis research questions. If the answer to either question is yes, then as scholars and professionals we must ask ourselves, might it not be embarrassing to get to the day after the next catastrophic attack and have to ask ourselves, "Why didn't we at least try to make it work?"

In the next two chapters this thesis will analyze the research completed and viable public policy options available.

THIS PAGE INTENTIONALLY LEFT BLANK

III. ANALYSIS AND FINDINGS

"However beautiful the strategy, you should occasionally look at the results."

—Sir Winston Churchill,
former prime minister of the United Kingdom

A. METHODOLOGY

The DHS Risk Management Framework provided in the National Infrastructure Protection Plan (NIPP) establishes the steps to combine consequence, vulnerability, and threat information to generate a rational assessment of national or sector risk. The national objective is to weigh infrastructure security priorities, goals, and requirements to allocate security resources effectively in order to reduce vulnerability, deter threats, and minimize the consequences of attacks.[182] With the NIPP model as the larger framework, the concepts used to construct the analytical decision framework in this thesis were derived from a thorough review of the literature on terrorist psychology, security technology, comparative security, and cost-benefit analysis formula and theory.

For use in responding to the first research question, quantitative data such as patron attendance and media exposure to sporting events and SEAR 4–5 events data was examined. Qualitative comparison was employed and examined doctrinal gaps and potential vulnerabilities which were revealed in the baseline literature review and public policies. The second research question was addressed using a cost-benefit analysis formula that was established in Mueller's "Terrorism, Security, and Money." The factors for the cost-benefit analysis also were derived from the literature, and sources for expense estimates are referenced in the analysis. For the third research question, this thesis proposes innovative ideas and revisits those presented in the literature for HSE consideration and potential working group research and development.

---

[182] Georgios Giannopoulos, Roberto Filippini, and Muriel Schimmer, *Risk Assessment Methodologies for Critical Infrastructure Protection: Part I, A State of the Art* (Luxembourg: Publications Office of the European Union, 2012), 34–35.

The literature review reflects an absence of direct, effective study of SEAR 4–5 event security in light of rapid 21st century changes in material circumstances that are enhancing their value as terrorist targets. To develop solutions, this thesis will analyze several key concepts. Consistent with PPD-8 strategy, the "whole of community" approach will be examined, including public-private collaboration for providing venue security operations, compliance inspections, and funding. The nexus among them set the context and direction for this chapter's analysis.

The cost-benefit analysis will determine grounds for the affordability of public policy action. The qualitative review will examine the gaps in the current HSE organizational structure, especially using comparative analysis of the experience of other nations. Upon thorough analysis, the synthesized findings will produce new considerations regarding the feasibility of direct government involvement, the indirect provision of government incentives, or as an alternative, the possible existence of other low-cost, advantageous courses of action for SEAR 4–5 sporting events.

B.   RESEARCH QUESTION 1

How well is the current National Protection Framework (the status quo) providing counterterrorism protection at sporting events in light of a) increasing media coverage at SEAR 4–5 events, and b) more rigorous protection at SEAR 1–3 events?

Even though the Boston Marathon was a SEAR 3 event, there are a vast majority of events at the SEAR 4–5 level that attract more patrons and viewers than do the collective total of SEAR 1–3 events. As an example of the massive scope of public vulnerability to attack, each week throughout the autumn months more than 1.1 million Americans attend SEAR 4 rated National Football League (NFL) games at 16 different venues nationwide and more than 3.4 million Americans attend college football games at more than three hundred SEAR 4 and 5 rated venues.[183]

This topic was briefly addressed in the Introduction and Literature Review, but due to the importance of select data trends to the theme of this thesis, certain aspects bear

---

[183] Gary Johnson, "NCAA Attendance Hits New High." *NCAA.com.* January 26, 2012. http://www.ncaa.com/news/football/article/2012-01-26/ncaa-attendance-hits-new-high.

reason for further examination in this Analysis chapter. This section of the chapter will be organized into four components to synthesize the conclusion:

- Data Trends: Terrorism Strategy, Tactics, and the Threat to Sporting Events
- Effect of Hardened Protective Posture at SEAR 1–3 events
- Effect of the National Protection Framework and Voluntary Best Practices
- 21st Century Circumstances rendering SEAR 4–5 Events as more Prominent

The purpose for addressing and resolving the first research question is to establish recent data reflects that SEAR 4–5 events are not only viable, valuable, and vulnerable soft targets but that it is wise to anticipate they will be attacked in the near future.

1. Data Trends: Terrorism Strategy, Tactics, and the Threat to Sporting Events

Though the literature review in Chapter II revealed the sociological factors of why sporting events make viable terrorist targets, and the marked history linking them, this section will analyze data to examine trends reflecting SEAR 4–5 venues as reasonably likely future targets.

Examining suicide-bombing attacks reveals that from 1990 through 1999 there were only 106 such terrorist assaults in fifteen different countries that claimed the lives of over 1,500 people. In comparison, from 2000 until 2010, there were 2,114 suicide-bombing attacks in thirty-two different countries that murdered more than 26,000 people.[184] In 2011 such attacks occurred in more than 70 countries world-wide,[185] accounting for 2,670 deaths.[186] Although suicide bombing attacks accounted for only 2.7 percent of all terrorist attacks that year, they accounted for 21 percent of the deaths related to terrorist attacks.[187] Fatalities, property damage, tremendous economic impact

---

[184] Moghaddam, *From the Terrorists' Point;* Jeffrey W. Lewis, *The Business of Martyrdom: A History of Suicide Bombing* (Annapolis, Md.: Naval Institute Press, 2012), 178, 346.

[185] Robert Anthony Pape and James K. Feldman, *Cutting the Fuse: The Explosion of Global Suicide Terrorism and How to Stop It.* 9Chicago: University of Chicago Press, 2010), 2, 349.

[186] Lewis, *The Business of Martyrdom,* 178, 346.

[187] U.S. National Counterterrorism Center, *2011 NCTC Report on Terrorism* (Washington, DC: National Counterterrorism Center, 2011), 13.

to the sports entertainment industry as well as the national economy, and a severely damaged faith in homeland security would be the expected consequences of a successful thoroughly planned suicide terrorism campaign targeting sports venues in America.[188]

One tactical reason for the global increase in suicide-bomb attack frequency is that it constitutes a very primitive form of "smart bomb." Terrorist planners value the ability for a dispatched attacker to visually identify and assess the target's security measures and be able to redirect to softer targets at the site if necessary.[189] A more strategic reason for their increased frequency is that suicide terrorism conveys an image of strength for a cause and defeat of a nation's security enterprise while building solidarity among its group members and followers.[190] The effects of a synchronized suicide bombing campaign at America's sporting events would convey superiority over the HSE while having historic and astronomical economic effects.

Another devastatingly effective terrorist strategy is to employ numerous coordinated bombings at a single target site, or simultaneously over a vast geographic area. Two of the deadlier terrorist attacks in Europe within the past decade were in Madrid (2004) and London (2005). The Spanish train bombings and English "7/7" attack were both the result of the tactic to use multiple, simultaneous detonations in public places of mass gathering.[191] Such a complex, synchronized attack of planting multiple IEDs at soft target sports venues across the country would have a similar deleterious effect on the American people and change the landscape of sports entertainment and venue security forever, further inhibiting American freedoms and civil liberties.

Several factors influence terrorist attack methods and tactics which, in turn, directly matter to the HSE protection of SEAR 4–5 venues. Though the most recent sports-related bombing at the Boston Marathon was not a suicide bombing, records

---

[188] Richard Fleece, "Suicide Terrorism in America?: The Complex Social Conditions of this Phenomenon and the Implications for Homeland Security" (Master's thesis, Naval Postgraduate School, December 2012).

[189] Hoffman, "Defending America," 21–22.

[190] Fleece, "Suicide Terrorism in America?"

[191] "IED Attack: The Danger," U.S. Department of Homeland Security (DHS).accessed January 12, 2014, http://www.dhs.gov/ied-attack-danger.

reflect that it was considered by the attackers but was an option they chose not to execute. This indicates the real presence of suicide bombing as a possible terrorist planning measure in America today. Further, terrorist tactics are related to security defense measures. As previously cited, suicide attacker "smart" bombers have the capability to analyze sporting venue protections at the site of the target and effect last minute decisions selecting exact detonation locations. In addition to suicide attackers, those planting IEDs, such as at the Boston Marathon, can also render last minute decisions about event venue vulnerabilities. This tactical agility possessed by the terrorists must be matched by the HSE in its protection mission capabilities.

This is important to SEAR 4–5 venue protection because it reflects the expanding possibility of different groups taking up arms at less orthodox times and places than perhaps currently anticipated by the Homeland Security Environment (HSE).

A number of other reasons, including logistical and economic factors, cause sporting events to be conducive to terror attacks. Among the enticing features for terrorist attacks, sports venues are in close proximity to transportation centers for use as escape routes. Additionally, they have far-reaching economic repercussions on the community around the stadium. Finally, the nature of the sporting events means inviting onto the premises masses of people about which the organizers know nothing.[192] Putting these reasons together with the opportunity to feed off of the "fear culture," terrorists often choose bombings and target places where people congregate such as transportation centers, sports stadiums, or related places.[193]

Thus, it can be safely asserted that terrorists are 1) motivated to deploy attacks to new targets in order to circumvent existing security measures, 2) considering soft targets and non-combatants as justifiable to attack, and 3) recognizing that American sports venues are symbolic icons of citizens trusting in their government for protection at these places of public gathering. As this relates to SEAR 4–5 sporting events, it is important to

---

[192] Tarlow, *Event Risk Management and Safety,* 135–137.

[193] Toohey, "Terrorism," 433.

recognize the types of terrorists that may plan and execute such an attack while linking their existence to a need for heightened security at the venue site.

In the past decade, the attacks of MAJ Nidal Hassan and the Tsarnaev brothers have been the most lethal and widely publicized terrorist attacks in America, both the result of home-grown radicalism. Both attacks were against soft targets to which these terrorists gained easy access demonstrating not only the ability, but the prevailing current tactic, to recognize soft targets at the local level that can be used as a platform for a terrorist cause.

Before analyzing the current protection mission doctrine and the materializing effects of some specific 21st century factors on SEAR 4–5 venues, it is instructive to review the effect of the enhanced security measures at America's SEAR 1–3 events as they relate to the lower-rated SEAR events.

2. Effect of Hardened Protective Posture at SEAR 1–3 events

Schütz remarks that the world's 21st century mega-sporting events, which capture hundreds of millions of spectators via television and Internet viewers, have opened an opportunity for host nations and cities to demonstrate "an unrivalled platform . . . to create an image of stability, openness, and prosperity."[194] This image is the cornerstone for building a positive and safe image for potential investors, business partners, and the tourism industry to elicit visitors and capital.[195] With the stability established, the host-nation's most highly prestigious foot forward, and security assured, these events serve as a catalyst for long-term economic reward.[196] Because the safe, successful completion of these events garner praise and benefit for the host nations, the disruption of them becomes a symbol of terrorist strength and the fortitude of their cause.

---

[194] Philip Schütz et al., *Smart Surveillance*, 2.

[195] Ibid.

[196] Ibid.

In the United States the Olympics are classified as an NSSE.[197] As cited in the Introduction, such events merit the most sophisticated CT strategic planning and surveillance technologies in the world. Because of the increasing trend in terrorism and late 20th century increased attraction for terrorists to attack high visibility sports venues, mega-events such as the Olympics and the Super Bowl have become veritable fortresses.

Following the success of the Munich attacks, security at the Olympics and other iconic sporting mega-events, like the soccer World Cup, were drastically solidified. The 1976 Games in Montreal were renowned for the draconian, prison camp-like security measures used to secure the athletes. Though not as rigid on the athletes now, Olympic security has often been regarded as the supreme model for event maximum security. It has become an ultimate staging point for newly developed technologies, information sharing, and tens of thousands of armed security personnel to provide protection. With the newest technologies tested and seemingly limitless security budgets, these mega-events have become consummate prototypes of sporting event security.

Security funding spent for the Games has been steadily, dramatically increasing over the decades since Munich.[198] For the London 2012 Games, the security costs reached $771 million and the costs for the 2014 Sochi Games are projected to eclipse the $3.2 billion mark. Whereas these weeks-long sporting events held at multiple venues incur the highest security costs, the NFL Super Bowl sustains proportionately higher security costs for the one day, single venue event. Completing the protection mission with SEAR 1 security measures at the 2014 Super Bowl in New Jersey cost $17.7 million.

It is clear that NSSEs and SEAR 1–3 events in America are proving secure largely as a result of receiving vast federal financial and operational support. However, there is an unforeseen consequence of these events becoming impenetrable (i.e., that terrorists will pivot to softer SEAR 4–5 event targets). This consequence is the result of the

---

[197] "National Special Security Events," U.S. Secret Service, accessed April 5, 2014, http://www.secretservice.gov/nsse.shtml, citing the Presidential Protection Act of 2000, Title 18, USC § 3056 which codified Presidential Decision Directive (PDD) 62

[198] United Kingdom, Department of Culture, Media and Sport, *London 2012 Olympic and Paralympic Games Quarterly Report—October 2012*, UK: United Kingdom, Department of Culture, Media and Sport, October 2012, http://uk.eurosport.yahoo.com/news/london-2012-final-cost-london-2012-games-revealed-135956051.html.

phenomenon of criminal activity "displacement." In the U.K. and U.S., although wide use of CCTV cameras in neighborhoods has had a deterrent effect there, crime has also "moved," or increased in other neighborhoods nearby that did not have cameras. This is the understandable concept that once potential perpetrators of crime recognize they are under surveillance, and are therefore suspect of either real-time reaction forces or a record of events for future judicial use, that criminal activity in that location decreases.

This same phenomenon is displayed in terrorist strategic and tactical innovations. As explained early in Chapter II, terrorist agility to adapt strategically and tactically means that the HSE agility must be equal or superior. The examples cited by Crenshaw were prior to the 9/11 attacks. The September 2001 attacks were simultaneously demonstrative of the strategic shift, to attack the West, and they were equally reflective of a tactical innovation to use airliners for more than ransom purposes, but rather, now as guided missiles.

Such tactical innovations were also reflected by the trends in the recorded terrorist activity regarding NSSE level Olympic Games and World Cup events in the past several decades. Since the 1972 Games there have been no successful attacks at the venue sites themselves. Rather, the successful attacks that resulted in the heaviest casualties were outside of the Games or World Cup matches, and took place at social gathering places of viewers and patrons.

In 1994, terrorists in Djibouti and Ulster claimed the lives of 10 spectators and wounded 20 others gathered at respective World Cup viewing events.[199] For the 2010 World Cup held in South Africa, two al-Shabaab suicide bombers struck a viewing crowd in Uganda while several attacks of viewers in Somalia led to a total of 77 deaths, 70 wounded and one hostage situation. The group Hizbul al Islam claimed responsibility for the attacks in Somalia claiming that it was a violation of Islamic law merely to gather to watch the sporting event.[200] Another three were slain, and 100 wounded in the 1996 Centennial Square bombing in downtown Atlanta, away from the sporting venues. These

---

[199] National Consortium for the Study of Terrorism and Responses to Terrorism (START), *Background Report: Terrorism and the Olympics Attacks* (College Park, MD: START, July 2012), 4.

[200] Ibid.

attacks and casualties can be in part attributed to the strength of the protective security measures in place at the sporting mega-events, yielding a form of Displacement. This is very relevant to SEAR 4–5 sporting matches as they are the logical alternative event targets to the heavily secured top-level SEAR venues.

Further reflecting terrorists' strategic planning flexibility to redirect to attack softer targets in the face of overwhelming site security, Faud Al-Shameli, planner for the 1972 Munich attack, stated that the mere bombing of an El Al (Israeli Airline) office is not enough. "We have to kill their most important and famous people. Since we cannot come close to their statesmen, we have to kill artists and sportsmen."[201] This also demonstrates that terrorists regard sporting events, athletes, spectators, or even selected corporate sponsors of sporting events as targets the result of Displacement from being able to attack higher profile figures.[202]

In this context then, the concept of criminal displacement may apply to the heavily secured SEAR 1–3 events, in effect enticing attacks upon SEAR 4–5 events. The logical inference is that as demonstrated with attacks moving to alternate locations away from heavily protected mega-events, so too terrorists may consider the lower rated SEAR events as softer targets worthwhile to attack. However, because the SEAR 1–3 events are outside of the notion of a steady-state, receiving support that is far beyond normal security measures, this thesis will next examine the National Protection Framework and the security industry Best Practices that coalesce to form America's security doctrine for SEAR 4–5 events.

3. Effectiveness of the National Protection Framework and Voluntary Best Practices

As revealed in the literature review, although DHS has not yet produced a National Protection Framework as a universally doctrinal expression of the current Administration's counterterrorism strategy, the working draft displays a vague overview of the topic. It does not provide specific examples of procedures, surveillance, and

---

[201] Toohey, "Terrorism," 434.

[202] Ibid., 438.

detection equipment to use, nor any standards for compliance regarding operations or staff training.

The Protection Framework is intended to be an overarching, strategic level document that takes specific ownership of sporting event venue security and defines the framework that encompasses NSSEs and SEAR events.[203] However, it does not delve into any particulars about site protection procedures, necessary equipment, training and compliance inspections, or funding. Nonetheless, pursuant to Presidential Policy Directive #8 (PPD-8), the Framework enumerates eight Core Capabilities for the Protection mission.[204] Six of the eight core capabilities are applicable to sports venue security: Intelligence and Information Sharing; Interdiction and Disruption; Screening, Search, and Detection; Access Control and Identity Verification; Physical Protective Measures; and Risk Management for Protection Programs and Activities.

Though these six capabilities are interwoven into one security scheme, two of them are intended to take place largely in preparation for events, namely, the Intel/info sharing and risk management planning. The remaining four capabilities are directly applicable at a venue. Physical protective measures and access/identity control are measures that security teams prepare for in advance of the events and can monitor during the events. It is in the last two core capabilities which the most challenges are presented because of their intrinsic reliance on real-time threat recognition and response. Screening and detection procedures will lead to search, interdiction, and disruption of operations on location.

However, in keeping with the framework's intent to establish a "flexible, scalable, and adaptable approach to the delivery" of PPD-8 Core Capabilities, the Framework is a generalized planning document. It is purposely not establishing readiness procedures or training standards and relinquishes the role of defining the decision making process and metrics to the SLLE and stakeholders.[205] Elsewhere in the framework, the Core

---

[203] FEMA, *Working Draft*, 2.

[204] Ibid., 12.

[205] Ibid., 7.

Capabilities are listed respectively with an accompanying set of bulleted Critical Tasks in an attempt to give more specific guidance beyond just the eight core capabilities. However, these critical tasks are only slightly less general than the Core Capabilities themselves.

In contrast to the higher level PPD and DHS Overview documents that are predicated on the imminent threat being known, the Protection Framework does address a doctrinal context when threat of attack is not imminent, by separating out a "Steady-State" status as opposed to the "Enhanced Steady-State."[206] Therefore, there is a discrepancy in national guidance to lower level events because NSSEs and SEAR 1–3 events receive federal support and do not constitute a steady state. In conclusion, the PPD level guidance does not accurately pertain to SEAR 4–5 events.

Nonetheless, despite this lack of inspection or compliance metric established at the federal level, achieving the core capabilities at the SLLE level was tied to federal funding. Using the core capability-based approach, the Protection Framework leaves it to the state/local level for inspection, evaluation, and reporting to FEMA as the DHS lead agency for national policy and guidance.

However, the effectiveness of the core capabilities-based approach has been called into question. DHS has attempted to link dollars spent to achieve the core capabilities but without established metrics or a proven system of inspection, compliance verification, or evaluation that is externally verifiable. The Government Accountability Office (GAO) found that FEMA lacked any standardization for data collection and overall data reliability yielding critical problems in its metrics and assessment process.[207] Therefore, there is room for alternative options to be raised that have already been proven effective.

Among the questions still to be resolved are whether adoption of the management system preparedness standards should be mandated, perhaps tied to federal funding, and how certification or accreditation against the standards would be conducted. The question

---

[206] Ibid., 27.

[207] Caudle, "Homeland Security," 9

also remains whether such a compliance and evaluation system can be effectively implemented to ensure the building and sustaining of core capabilities if it is only voluntary.[208] This is especially valid when considering the source of the answer to fill the void of doctrine for SEAR 4–5 events, the various and unsynchronized Best Practice documents.

Over the past decade there has been an inordinate number of best practice-type documents developed from various sources and levels of the HSE. The origins range from professional and college levels of the sports entertainment industry to select government or non-government organizations. As an example, in 2005, the Department of Justice (DoJ) produced "Planning and Managing Security for Major Special Events: Guidelines for Law Enforcement."[209] In the same year, DHS (via FEMA) produced "Special Events Contingency Planning: Job Aids Manual."[210] Both were voluminous documents that explored issues for terrorist attack and non-terrorist based safety issues. The result was two federal agencies producing versions of doctrine on the same subject without proper coordination. Further, because one document was produced at DoJ and one at DHS, there developed a discrepancy in distribution, reference, usage, and compliance.

However, one strategic planning concept was introduced in the 2005 DoJ "Major Special Event: Guidelines" that is still widely in use for special event security. The site location strategy entails establishing three concentric rings of security, an outer ring, a middle ring, and an inner ring. The intent is for the security to get progressively more rigorous moving from outer to inner ring.[211] However, this strategy is routinely only applied to "major events" (i.e., the NSSEs and SEAR 1–3 events). The same conceptual

---

[208] Ibid., 10

[209] Edward Connors, *Planning and Managing Security for Major Special Events: Guidelines for Law Enforcement* (Alexandria, VA: Institute for Law and Justice, March 2005).

[210] Department of Homeland Security, Federal Emergency Management Agency, "Special Events Contingency Planning: Job Aids Manual," (Washington, DC: FEMA, March 2005).

[211] Connors, *Planning and Managing Security*, 33–37.

site counterterrorism posture is successfully practiced abroad in Israel and employs interlocking defensive layers to identify and track a threat for subsequent interdiction.[212]

Since 2005, scholarly and NGO sources have emerged as well to produce well-regarded venue security Best Practices. The University of South Carolina produces the Journal of Event Venue and Management (JEVM), and the Sports Entertainment Venue Tomorrow (SEVT) annual conference, both of which include various professionals from throughout the field to discuss Best Practices for management and security issues. Likewise, the National Center for Spectator Sports Safety and Security (NCS4) at Southern Mississippi University routinely produces publications and conducts an annual summit that also addresses Best Practices for security.

One sports venue stakeholder issuing Best Practice-type guidance was the National Collegiate Athletic Association (NCAA). It issued "planning options" as guidelines for intercollegiate athletic programs but there have not been any requisite standards in place for institutions to adhere to or be held accountable for by the NCAA or local law enforcement. Therefore, there is a lack of consistency in security management practices at university sports events throughout the United States.[213] The National Football League has also produced a best practices guide that has since been adapted for use with other professional sports leagues. But currently none of the best practices are required by the federal government in order to meet a facility licensing or staff certification standard. Since there is no federal inspection or compliance process, their implementation is voluntary. This reveals the possibility that many facilities and organizations may not be implementing even the suggested practices.

Synthesizing previous research conducted is relevant to the analysis in this thesis. Post 9/11 heightened security measures were increasingly seen as problematic to venue and event managers as early as in 2002.[214] It was also revealed that as early as 2003

---

[212] Nadav Morag, *Homeland Security in Israel: Counterterrorism Strategies* (Monterey, CA: Naval Postgraduate School, Center for Homeland Defense and Security, 2011).

[213] Hall et al., "Securing Collegiate Sport Stadiums," 1

[214] Hurst, Pratsinakis, and Zoubek, "American Sports."

football stadiums generally scored higher in security surveys than basketball facilities.[215] Important to this thesis, several reasons for the disparity included such causes as the volume of basketball events leading to higher security costs at arenas than at football stadiums, and the general perception that the arena facility was "just another building" on campus.[216] This reflected a trend of growing complacency amid facility security operations linked to event frequency and cost.[217] This trend continued to worsen in time. In 2007, 87% of football facility managers had an established emergency action plan in place, but only 75% of them had actually ever practiced it.[218] Meanwhile, intercollegiate facility managers strongly agreed that terrorism is a foreseeable threat and that terrorist activity at a collegiate sports venue was not a matter of if, but when it will occur.

Also that same year, DHS analyzed commonalities or trends in mission critical shortcomings at various collegiate sports venues. The end product would identify weaknesses for management to then harden the venue security. They conducted unannounced game day audits to ensure measures said to be in place actually were in place and found there was a lack of consistency in security management practices at university sports events throughout the United States.[219] The litany of security task failures included:

- Porous perimeter control
- Failing physical protection systems
- Loose venue and facility access control
- Insufficient security team and venue staff training
- Non-existent communications in the stadium and with local first responders
- Inadequate emergency response and evacuation plans

---

[215] M. Pantera et al., "Best Practices for Game Day Security at Athletic & Sport Venues." *The Sport Journal* 6, no. 4 (2003). http://www.thesportjournal.org/article/best-practices- game-day-security-athletic-sport.

[216] Pantera et al., "Best Practices."

[217] Hall et al., "Securing Collegiate Sport Stadiums."

[218] John Miller and Adam Dunn, "Perceptions of Terrorist Threat: Implications for Intercollegiate Basketball Venue Managers," *Journal of Venue and Entertainment Management* 3, no. 1 (July 2011): 3.

[219] Hall et al., "Securing Collegiate Sport Stadiums," 1.

- Inconsistent pre-event searching of facilities
- Fluctuating standards for searches of fans and their belongings
- No accountability for vendors and their vehicles
- Concession areas not secured with intrusion detection systems
- Absence of closed-circuit television (CCTV) in and around the stadiums[220]

By 2011, even though 87% of the arena managers indicated they had an emergency plan in place in the event of terrorist attack, which was consistent with 2007 surveys, now only 46% conducted counter-terrorism contingency training with their staffs.[221] Furthermore, of those that did conduct training, most of them, only 18% in total were conducting training once annually. By meeting perfunctorily only once per year, it is logical that staff members may lose a sense of urgency for counterterrorism preparation or focus for providing a safe environment. Thus, the trend in venue staff terrorist event training had consistently declined from 2002 to 2011[222]

Another troubling trend that developed by 2011, was that a majority of facility managers were not adjusting their risk management and security posture in accordance with the DHS alert system increases.[223] The final disturbing factor was that in that same year, only one third of the nation's 1,350 sports arenas and stadiums were providing improved security compared to 1990s era operational practices.[224] Thus, it is evident that although facility managers perceive the terrorist threat as real, they do not have confidence in their doctrine or training levels. Additionally, complacency, funding, and resources are common constraints preventing them from applying enhanced measures. In general, the security teams at the two-thirds of sporting venues are little or no better prepared to protect the public against terrorism attacks than they were prior to the 2001 attacks.[225]

---

[220] Ibid.

[221] Miller and Dunn, "Perceptions of Terrorist Threat."

[222] Ibid.: Goss, Jubenville, and MacBeth, *Transatlantic Implications*.

[223] Miller and Dunn, "Perceptions of Terrorist Threat."

[224] Keating, "Industry of Fear."

[225] Ibid.

While the media exposure or public visibility of the event is certainly a significant factor for terrorists to consider in target selection, complacency in implementing security best practices rendering them extremely soft targets to attack also weighs into terrorist operational decision making processes.

As has been demonstrated throughout this thesis, large public gatherings, such as sports events, that celebrate American popular culture are considered terrorist targets. In the 21st century, sports managers must be adequately trained and knowledgeable of available security measures in order to prepare for, prevent, detect, and deter potential threats to their sports venues. The HSE goal is to increase capabilities, to match terrorist innovative planning agility, and to more efficiently protect from acts of terrorism and exercise crowd management. In sum, however, the voluntary Best Practice-type documents, which serve as the de facto doctrinal sports venue security standards for the government, are failing.

4.   **21st Century Circumstances Rendering SEAR 4–5 Events As More Prominent**

Over the past half century there has been a dramatic increase in global and national terrorist attacks. As noted in Chapter II, there were 168 sports-related terrorist events between 1972–2004 to assert the strong ties between terrorism and sports.[226] Of relevance to SEAR 4–5 event venues is that facility managers whose institutions hosted the top 100 attended NCAA basketball programs in 2011, 15% of them knew of terrorist threats at their universities and 10% of them had received terrorist threats at their own facility.[227] These were all SEAR 4–5 rated event venues. The largest demographic of these 100 facility managers possessed more than 10 years of experience in their jobs, demonstrating that they were not inexperienced or insecure in their positions.

Meanwhile, as attendance and complacency has been increasing at SEAR 4–5 events, standards have been decreasing. ESPN, MLB, and other available public sources from the nation's sporting leagues and conferences reveal that attendance in the sport of

---

[226] Toohey, "Terrorism," 433.

[227] Miller and Dunn, "Perceptions of Terrorist Threat," 1.

baseball and college football (both SEAR 4–5 events) has steadily increased over the past 50 years. This increase in attendance is a very relevant factor for terrorist targeting selection. However, to begin putting event venue attendance figures in perspective, it is important to raise the concern that possibly even the U.S. HSE may not have an accurate appreciation of crowd sizes at SEAR 4–5 events.

For example, the smallest average attendance crowd in MLB games (Tampa, 18,645) is nearly double the average attendance for a major league soccer match in Scotland (10,263) and approaches the level of the average attendance for a major league soccer match in Italy (19,968).[228] The Tampa baseball games are SEAR 4 or 5 events. As another example, the Dayton Dragons lead Minor League Baseball's lowest professional league in attendance per game (8,405), according to MiLB.com. Yet the attendance at the Dayton games is close to the average attendance of a major league soccer match in Scotland, and is greater than one Major League Soccer team in Italy.[229] Furthermore, in Dayton, the club has sold out its venue for each of the season's 70 games for 14 straight years, according to MiLB.com. The Dayton baseball games are SEAR 5 events. With figures such as these, it becomes increasingly apparent that in America, even our Minor League baseball games, held daily throughout the summer, can pose as large a public gathering target as many major league sporting events throughout Europe.

In analyzing attendance figures just within the United States, SEAR 4–5 events demonstrate sufficient suitability for terrorist attack to cause catastrophic casualty figures. Although Division I intercollegiate basketball facilities do not attract comparable crowds to mega-events such as the Olympics or Super Bowls, they possess abundant capacities to result in drastic casualties if they were to be the subject of an attack. In fact, it has been articulated that a sporting event does not need to have 70,000 fans in attendance in order to have significantly consequential effects.[230]

---

[228] "Italian Serie A Stats: Team Attendance—2013–14" and "Scottish Premier League Stats: Team Attendance - 2013–14," *ESPN FC*, accessed April 4, 2014, http://espnfc.com/stats/attendance/_/league/sco.1/scottish-premiership?cc=5901; http://espnfc.com/stats/attendance/_/league/ita.1/italian-serie-a?cc=5901

[229] "Italian Serie A Stats."

[230] Miller and Dunn, "Perceptions of Terrorist Threat," 2.

Delving into college basketball attendance statistics provides useful data: The top five individual team leaders in attendance during the 2009–2010 season were the University of Kentucky (24,111 per game), Syracuse University (22,152 per game), the University of Louisville (19,397 per game), the University of Tennessee (19,168 per game), and the University of North Carolina-Chapel Hill (17,786 per game), according to the National Collegiate Athletic Association (NCAA). The bottom five schools rounding out the top 100 during the same season were New Mexico State University (5,659 per game), the University of Northern Iowa (5,642 per game), Tulsa University (5,491 per game), Marshall University (5,481 per game), and the University of Central Florida (5,411 per game), according to the NCAA. Thus, the average attendance numbers of the top five schools during the 2009–2010 season was 20,523, while the average for the bottom five of the top 100 schools averaged 5,537 spectators per contest. Although these figures may pale in comparison to the attendance at NCAA football games, an organized attack could result in a death toll greater than the official death toll from the September 11, 2001 attacks of 2,977.[231]

Furthermore, another routine SEAR 4 event, MLB game attendance figures reflect a steady increase over the past 35years.[232] At 74,026,895, MLB total attendance is the most highly attended of any sporting league in the world. This is a total attendance that is 5.5 times that of the German Bundesliga (soccer), the next highest non-American sporting league, and 4.5 times that of the NFL. Though the MLB season plays more games than any other sport, the average game attendance is 30,504, ranking it fourth in the world only behind the NFL, Bundesliga, and England's Premier League (soccer).[233] All of the regular season MLB games are SEAR 4 events.

Even the baseball pre-season games played every year in March reflect valuable data demonstrating viability as significant soft targets. The overall MLB average for these pre-season games is similar to that of the regular season MiLB games, and again, is

---

[231]Ibid.

[232] *Associated Press,* "MLB Attendance Drops 1.2 Percent This Year," *USA Today,* October 1, 2013, http://www.usatoday.com/story/sports/mlb/2013/10/01/mlb-attendance-drops-12-percent-this-year/2904661/.

[233] "MLB Attendance Report—2013," *ESPN,* accessed October 17, 2013. http://www.espn.go.com/mlb/attendance.

similar to the data reflected at major league sporting events in Europe. The league average is 6,745 attendees and the team which commands the highest attendance is the world-renowned New York Yankees franchise. The Yankees games average 10,300 people per pre-season game. It is imperative to note that teams play 16–18 games per pre-season in small, virtually unprotected soft target venues in Arizona and Florida.[234] Making these soft targets pre-season MLB venues even more appealing as terror targets is that they also represent a significant boost to local economies. In Florida alone, pre-season baseball adds $753 million to the local economy each year.[235] These pre-season games are attended by many spectators that electively travel and take their vacations to Florida in the spring. A successful campaign of multiply coordinated terrorist attacks at these virtually unprotected soft targets could have a devastatingly crushing effect on the local economies for many years to come.

Because these smaller SEAR 4–5 venues are highly vulnerable and offer rewarding opportunities for terrorists to plan them as targets, this section will briefly reflect on the effects of IEDs and the possibility that bomb attacks on smaller, softer targets can be as deadly or deadlier than at the larger SEAR 1–3 venues.

Various DHS and U.S. military sources demonstrate that damage caused by IEDs depend on their size, content, construction, and placement.[236] As expected, because vehicles can be a larger platform on which to carry explosive material, they can do more damage.[237] Therefore, even the stadium parking lots are perhaps more vulnerable than inside the ballparks because of their relative weakness in security with little or no use of security cameras or vehicle inspection systems to access the lots.

---

[234] Grapefruit, Cactus Leagues See Average Spring Training Attendance Drop," *Sports Business Daily*, April 5, 2013, http://www.sportsbusinessdaily.com/Daily/Issues/2013/04/05/Research-and-Ratings/Spring-Training.aspx.

[235] "Florida Grapefruit League - 2013 Attendance, "Florida Grapefruit League, http://www.floridagrapefruitleague.com/home/attendance/.

[236] DHS, "IED Attack."

[237] Ibid.

Figure 3.   Georgia Dome Tailgate Party; Effects of Marriott Car Bomb Attack[238]

Venue parking lots, as shown in Figure 3, are renowned for hosting social gatherings and "tailgate" parties for American pro and collegiate football, auto racing, soccer and a myriad of other sporting and concert events. The parking lots are frequented annually by as many as 240 million American tailgaters that spend $35 billion on everything from food and beverages to tents and barbecue equipment.[239]   These figures reflect just for the social events in the parking lots before and after the sporting events. Therefore, stadium bowls are not the only potential terrorist target but parking lots and tailgating events are also potential terrorist targets. Figure 3 depicts a typical crowded tailgate party outside a SEAR 4 sporting event venue and displays a 33 foot deep by 40 foot wide crater caused by the 2008 Islamabad Hotel car bomb that killed 60 people and injured 260. The 2,000 lb. VBIED responsible for this damage could be housed in a small box truck or even a full-sized SUV or van, like the ones shown in Figure 3.

As indicated earlier, the vulnerability of these venues has increased with the globalization of communications, which has facilitated the posting of instructional material pertaining to bomb construction and placement by jihadist and terrorist groups across the globe. As a by-product of the war in Iraq, now there also is massive quantities

---

238 Photo sources: Jason Getz, "Falcons Tailgating Rules," *Atlanta Journal Constitution*; August 8, 2013; Bill Roggio, "Bombing at Islamabad Marriott Latest in String of Complex Terror Attacks," *CBS News Photo*, September 21, 2008.

239 "Tailgating: Behind the Numbers," *SportsBusiness Daily*, November 2012, http://www.sportsbusinessdaily.com/SB-Blogs/Events/Motorsports-Marketing-Forum/2012/11/Nascar-Tailgate-Graphic.aspx.

of online reviews analyzing bomb attacks and IED technology of differing sizes and delivery methods. The Boston Marathon Bombing demonstrated that these sources are being used by potential attacks by home-grown radicals.

Providing a further challenge to the HSE, DHS sources also reflect that the domestic terrorism bomb attacks in Oklahoma City and at the Atlanta Olympics, two of the most notorious perpetrated in the United States, were made or effectively compounded with simple homemade materials.[240] The combination of the available materials with the "How To" on-line instructions, poses a serious threat to America's HSE.

Citing the multiple effects and injuries resulting from bomb blasts, it is relevant to note that the type and number of injuries will vary depending on the physical environment and the size of the blast, the amount of shielding between victims and the blast, fires, or resulting structural damage, and whether the explosion occurs in an enclosed space or an open area such as an outdoor ballpark.[241] Germane to this thesis are the bomb blast effects which vary according to the size and structure of the sporting venues.

Not surprisingly, a review of architectural layouts and plans available from MLB and MiLB reveal that the structural dimensions of minor league stadiums are smaller than major league baseball parks. However, though smaller, they may offer a tactically superior selection as a terrorist target.

Routinely, minor league baseball stadiums do not have seating areas in the outfield portion of the venue as opposed to the much larger MLB stadiums.[242] This means that the attendees in the smaller stadium will produce a more closely seated audience as opposed to attendees seated in a larger, emptier stadium with the same or similar size audience. Thus, the MiLB ballparks will very possibly yield a higher concentration of individuals in a smaller area. Therefore, the more densely populated stadium crowd will result in a higher death and casualty toll from the attack.

---

[240] DHS, "IED Attack."

[241] Ibid.

[242] "Prince George's Stadium," *MiLB.com,* accessed April 4, 2014, http://www.milb.com/content/page.jsp?sid=t418&ymd=20090311&content_id=522855&vkey=team1

Figure 5 illustrates this point. The same bomb blast amid 7,000 fans in the Prince George's Stadium, home of the Bowie Baysox AA baseball club, will more likely result in higher casualty figures than 7,000 fans dispersed through the larger Baltimore Orioles ballpark at Camden Yards (Figure 4). Consequently, the casualties produced by the same single detonated IED in a smaller, more crowded stadium can possibly reign more bomb blast effect and causal damage than in a lesser crowded, larger stadium.[243] Therefore, there exists a realistic possibility that the effects of a bomb blast in the routinely sold-out minor league stadium in Dayton would score more casualties than in the routinely less than half full major league stadium in Tampa. For these reasons, the stadium in Dayton may become the target of choice for an astute terrorist, with the attack there bearing the lower risk of being thwarted while likely accomplishing the goal of a higher casualty impact.

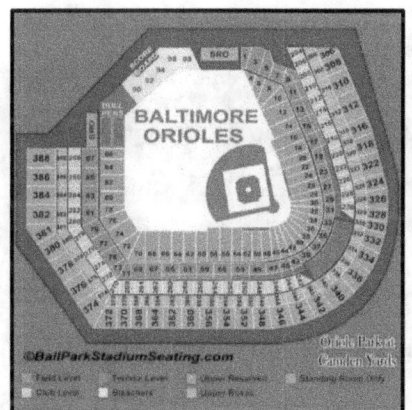 

Figure 4.   MLB Stadium "Camden Yards" Seating Diagram and Aerial Photo[244]

---

[243] U.S. Department of Homeland Security (DHS), "Bomb Threat Stand-off Chart," March 20, 2009, https://www.llis.dhs.gov/sites/default/files/DHS-BombThreatChart-6-5-09.pdf.

[244] Photos from BallParkSatiumsSeating.com, http://www.ballparkstadiumseating.com/oriole-park-at-camden-yards-seating-chart-view-map/; "Stadium Travel Guide: Baltimore," http://www.stadiumtravelguide.com/baseball/baltimore.htm.

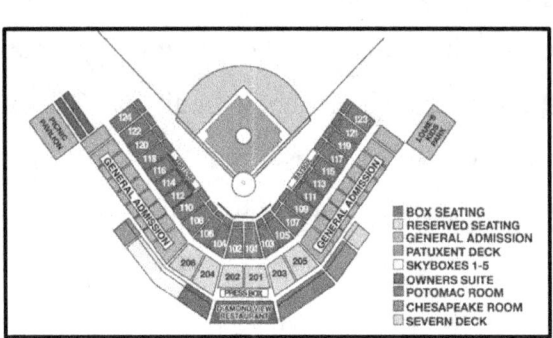 

Figure 5.   MiLB "Prince George's Stadium" Seating Diagram and Rooftop Photo[245]

These smaller, minor league, or SEAR 5 venues are often located in smaller communities and less urban areas. Because of this, local Emergency Response teams may not be as large, as well funded, or aptly trained for terrorism event responses as MLB stadiums. Further, because of the size of the security force at the smaller MiLB venue, if an attack includes multiple blasts, it will quickly tax the available security force, diverting them from efficient evacuation and response measures. Whereas at larger major league size venues, or at SEAR 1–3 venues, a significantly larger security team will likely have more capability to react to separate incidents and still execute various evacuation and crowd control measures.

Moreover, a known terrorist tactic is to attract bystanders to windows, doorways, and the outside with gunfire, small bombs, or other methods and then detonate a larger, more destructive device, significantly increasing human casualties.[246] Because these smaller venues may be older, or less well funded when constructed, they are more likely to have more narrow concourse levels and less efficient access and egress points from which to evacuate the stadium. This leads to the possibility of a congested exit route being the target of a secondary bomb.

[245] Photos from "Stadium Diagram," MiLB.com, http://ww.milb.com/content/page.jsp?sid=t418&ymd=20100328&content_id=8975064&vkey=team1; "The Monumental Experience," http://cherryhillpark.wordpress.com/tag/baltimore-orioles/.

[246] "Bomb-Threat Stand-Off Distances," U.S. National Counterterrorism Center (NCTC). Accessed April 4, 2014, http://www.nctc.gov/site/technical/bomb_threat.html.

The smaller, less funded, or older stadiums may also not be built with terrorism or bomb damage in mind unlike many of the newer major league stadiums now being built (e.g., Texas Stadium).[247] One of the prompts for this thesis is the premise that SEAR 5 level venues possess a smaller amount of current protective video and explosive trace detection technology than do the SEAR 1–3 venues. This means that with less 24/7 surveillance coverage in and around a stadium, an attacker may conduct reconnaissance of the location more easily and from closer range with less chance of being spotted by venue security teams.

Not only are SEAR 4–5 venue facilities soft targets that offer a high payoff benefit in casualties for terrorists to consider, but their exposure to the media and therefore, viewers and more citizens watching or listening, has also expanded dramatically in the past decade.

Catarina Kinnvall defines the concept of globalization that "events elsewhere [in the world] have consequences for our everyday political, social, and economic lives, affecting individuals' sense of being."[248] This means that more people in more places are noticing, or affected by more things happening, primarily because they are learning about them in real-time through the Internet and global media. Therefore, 21st century globalization enhances the effectiveness and value of terrorism strikes at smaller, historically perceived less noticeable venues.

Simultaneous to the increase in SEAR 4–5 event exposure through 21st century media and device platforms, the Nielsen company ratings reflect a long and steady decline in television ratings for the Olympic Games. This section of the thesis is not intended to imply that terrorists regard Nielsen ratings as a target selection consideration. However, the ratings are generally reflective of how much exposure a given event attains and therefore, how well it may serve as a platform for their cause. Prior to 1972, the Olympic Games had not been struck by terrorism. However, as discussed previously, it was these Munich Games which clearly established the modern day link of sports with terrorism.

---

[247] Anderson, "How Dallas Does Security."

[248] Kinnvall, "Globalization and Religious Nationalism," 742.

During the Munich Games, the extensive coverage of the PLO attack on the Israeli Olympic team was a watershed broadcasting moment in the history of 20th century terrorism, receiving a Nielsen rating of 20.9 and share of 45, according to the audience-measuring company. This equates to 21% of all televisions in America watching the broadcast while 45% of all televisions in use across the country during the time of the broadcast were watching it. As cited in the literature review, the PLO/BSO selected the Games to assault for internally opportunistic political reasons, but also because they were a soft target and televised around the world.

As a globally televised mega-event, the Olympics reached its zenith for television ratings in the 1970s, with the Games in Montreal only slightly higher than those in Munich. Since then there has been a marked steady decline in television ratings, Nielsen data show. This decline could be due to many factors such as time zones of the host nations, changes in association of political power with the events, the fall of Communism, etc. However, the bottom line reflected by the Nielsen ratings since 1976 is that as an event of mass appeal for consideration as a terrorist target, the numbers of viewers for the mega-event of the Olympics has drastically decreased. Meanwhile SEAR 4–5 events such as NFL and MLB games have shown a vastly marked increase in viewership in the 21st century.

Similarly, data reflect that the rating status of television viewership in America in general (i.e., the percent of all television-equipped homes watching a particular program at one time) is also clearly on a downward trend.[249] This means it is far less likely now for America, collectively, to be watching any one show or event at the same time. Over the past sixty years, the seasonal leader in average nightly television rating has gone from the "I Love Lucy" show's 67.3% of the market in 1952–53 to 12.3% of the market for NCIS in 2012–13.[250] This means that there was an 84% decrease in the phenomenon of

---

[249] Jim Edwards, "TV Is Dying, And Here Are The Stats That Prove It," *Business Insider*, November 24, 2013.

[250] Alex McNeil, *Total Television,* 4th ed (New York: Penguin, 1996); "2003-04 Season to Date Program Rankings from September 22, 2003, through May 30, 2004," *ABC Medianet*; Tim Brooks and Earle Marsh, *The Complete Directory to Prime Time Network and Cable TV Shows, 1946-Present* (New York: Ballantine Books), 1679–1698; Nellie Andreeva, "Full 2010–11 Season Series Rankings," *Deadline: Hollywood,* May 2, 2011.

Americans routinely watching the same show at the same time. The leading television show in the U.S. in 2011–12 was NBC's Sunday Night Football, at 12.9%. NFL Football is a SEAR 4 sporting event in America, and that television season it was routinely the most highly watched show in America.[251]

Continuing the trend of rapidly narrowing the gap in exposure in the media between global mega-events and the SEAR 4–5 events was most recently demonstrated with America's viewing of the 2014 Winter Olympics. The daily average television ratings were down 10% in 2014 from 2012, continuing the trend since the 1970s, according to Nielsen. Even one of the Olympics' usually largest television draws, the prime time telecast of the closing ceremonies lost out in the ratings to American Movie Channel network's series, "The Walking Dead."[252] However, despite dropping television numbers, the Sochi Olympics demonstrated the 21st century's growing reliance on and developing value in multiple forms of media to watch events, especially through on-line streaming.

For the first time ever a broadcasting company reported that it aired more hours via on-line streaming coverage than it aired on television. NBC also reported that its viewership on-line was up 54% from the 2010 Games. NBC asserts this is reflective of the "rapidly transforming [the] way people experience the event."[253] Although the daily average American TV audiences continued to trend downward, the overall viewership of the Games was boosted 20% by viewing via online streaming. The resulting trend is that the more devices that viewers are using to watch event is leading to overall elevations in the numbers of viewers for the sporting event. NBC's Allan Wurtzel observed, "A rising tide lifts all boats."

This trend is relevant to SEAR 4–5 events because this same form of marketing and media exposure has increased the exposure and visibility of such events, thereby

---

[251] Edwards, "TV Is Dying."

[252] Bill Brioux, "Olympic TV Ratings Down from Vancouver, but Online Numbers Soar: Daily TV Average Dropped from Four Million Viewers to 1.5 Million," *Canadian Press*, February 25, 2014. http://www.canada.com/entertainment/Olympic+ratings+down+from+Vancouver+online+numbers+soar/9549618/story.html.

[253] David Bauder, "Online offerings transform Olympic experience," *Associated Press*, February 12, 2014, http://wintergames.ap.org/article/online-offerings-transform-olympic-experience.

increasing their value as terrorist targets. Therefore, what the data trend reveals is a 21st century reality that it is no longer necessary to strike an Olympics or World Cup mega-event just to gain worldwide exposure for a terrorist cause when tremendous exposure can be gained globally by striking a much softer target such as a hotel[254] or soft target sporting event.[255]

Considering that terrorists plan their attacks to gain as much media exposure as possible,[256] the expansion of devices on which to watch sporting events, especially through the Internet, means that these heretofore non-broadcasted events are now widely seen and heard around the nation and the world. With the past decade's explosion of Internet and television network sports package marketing and innovations using accessible devices such as smartphones, iPads, tablets, and personal computers, the de-centralization of sports broadcasting has also enabled spectators to watch a greater variety of sports at an infinite variety of times.[257]

These SEAR 4–5 sporting events are now broadcast via the Internet and satellite radio in massively greater numbers than they were as little as a decade ago.

Sporting event venues are perfect sites for both large-scale and small-scale attacks, and the need for the mega-event such as the Olympics to serve as the terrorist sporting event platform of choice, is diminishing.[258] In this rapidly globalizing community, as part of the Counterterrorism campaign, sporting event risk managers "are not only on the front lines, but they are also warriors for peace."[259]

In less than its first decade, MLB's Internet-based subscription package viewership has risen from its inception to more than 3.9 million subscribers worldwide in

---

[254] Onook. Manish and Raghav, "Information Control," 33–43.

[255] Susan Candiotti "Suspect: Boston Bombing was Payback for Hits on Muslims," *CNN*, May 17, 2013, http://www.cnn.com/2013/05/16/us/boston-bombing-investigation/.

[256] Toohey, "Terrorism," 433.

[257] Alan Wurtzel, NBC Sports, February, 2014

[258] Tarlow, *Event Risk Management* ,135–137

[259] Ibid., XIII.

more than 60 nations.[260] Furthermore, since its inception on Jan. 1, 2009, there are an additional 70 million American households that have cable television packages including the MLB Network, which also broadcasts SEAR 4–5 MLB and MiLB games.[261]

This equates to one half million Americans attending soft target events nightly throughout the spring and summer months across the nation combined with approximately 5 million people watching and listening online or through satellite television and radio packages across the nation and the world. These widely broadcast baseball sporting events are soft targets and are routinely designated as SEAR 4–5 events.

MLB.TV now asserts it is available on more than 400 different forms of broadcast devices including video game systems and smart phones. This trend of expanding global communications shows no signs of changing. Swedish telecommunications company Ericsson projects that by 2019 there will be 5.6 billion smart phones and 9.3 cell phones in total throughout the world.[262] European research firm, Enders Analysis, projects that the number of smart phones in use worldwide will exceed the number of personal computers in the first half of 2014.[263]

Broadcasted visually on television and the Internet, MLB games are also broadcast live worldwide via satellite radio. Today, Sirius XM radio facilitates the broadcast of every MLB game and began 2014 with 25.56 million subscribers.[264] But this was not always the case. On 9/11, satellite radio broadcasting of sporting events was in its infancy. Demonstrated in the chart below is the accelerated growth of global satellite radio broadcasting (in numbers of millions of subscribers).

---

[260] Om Malik, "Happy Birthday MLB.TV. Now That's What I Call Sports TV," GIGAOM, August 26, 2012, http://gigaom.com/2012/08/26/happy-10th-birthday-mlb-tv-now-thats-what-i-call-sports-tv/.

[261] Robert Seidman, "List of How Many Homes Each Cable Network Is In—As of August 2013." *TV by the Numbers*, August 23, 2013.

[262] Associated Press, "Number of Smartphones Expected to Triple to 5.6 Billion by 2019," *Washington Time*s, November 11, 2013, http://www.washingtontimes.com/news/2013/nov/11/number-smartphones-expected-triple-56-billion-2019/.

[263] Henry Blodgett, "The Number of Smartphones in Use Is about to Pass the Number of PCs," *Business Insider*, December 11, 2013, http://www.businessinsider.com/number-of-smartphones-tablets-pcs-2013-12.

[264] "Sirius XM Exceeds 2013 Net Subscriber Target; Issues 2014 Subscriber And Free Cash Flow Guidance," SiriusXM, January 7, 2014, http://investor.siriusxm.com/releasedetail.cfm?ReleaseID=817666.

Year	Sirius	SiriusXM	XM	Note
2013		25.56		
2010		20.19		
2007	8.32	17.33	9.01	***
2004	1.14	4.24	3.1	**
2001			0.03	*

* GM begins factory installed XM Satellite radio
** Year Announced MLB Contract to start in 2005
*** Year of Sirius and XM Satellite Radio merger

Figure 6.   Growth of Satellite Radio Subscriptions[265]

The rapidly expanding radio listening numbers over the past decade from across the globe indicate the further exposure of MLB (SEAR 4) events beyond just that of the visual broadcasts on television and on-line.

Data reflect that the mega-events are spending immense amounts of money and committing vast numbers of security personnel to pose a much more difficult challenge for a terrorist to penetrate than ever before. Meanwhile, similar or greater casualty rates are attainable at the soft target venues. Coupled with the tremendously rapid increase of national and global coverage of NFL, MLB, MiLB or NCAA athletic events in real-time, from the terrorists' perspective, the phenomenon of Displacement is worthy of grave consideration, transforming these SEAR 4–5 venues into attractive targets.

C.   RESEARCH QUESTION 2

Are there quantitative or qualitative methods to demonstrate a positive cost-benefit relationship between potential solutions v. consequential alternatives?

1.   Definitions and Objectives

In this era of fiscal austerity, to recommend or even to propose public policy options that incur greater fiscal expense is difficult, if not hopeless. Therefore, this thesis

---

[265] "SiriusXM Reports 2012 Results," SiriusXM. February 5, 2013, http://investor.siriusxm.com/releasedetail.cfm?ReleaseID=737857.

will analyze and determine innovative concepts for venue security public policy options that are of little or no cost to the federal government, those that are already built into the DHS budget, and those that can be subsidized through public-private partnerships with concurrent citizen contribution to minimize federal expense. To explain the overall cost-benefit concept, Figure 7 provides an illustration of a basic economic model.

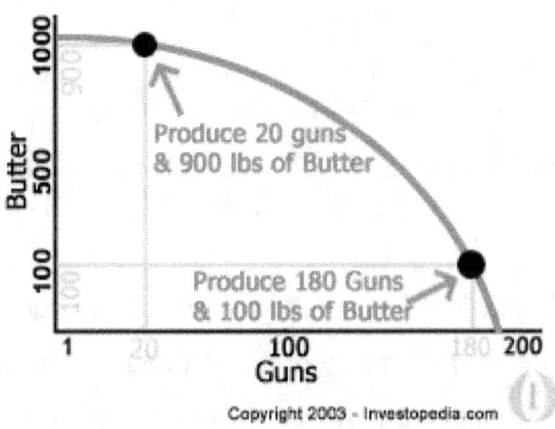

Figure 7.   Demonstrating a Macro-Economic Model of Expenditure Returns[266]

The timeless macro-economic challenge faced by government is to cyclically consider, decide, spend, and re-evaluate how much of its funding resources it wants to put toward the production of "guns v. butter." That principle applies with the government's annual decisions regarding the DOD or DHS/HSE budgets on defense and security spending as opposed to the plethora of other non-security-oriented domestic spending. In fiscally responsible governments, finite funding is allocated in order to conduct operations through a year. Therefore, the more money that is spent on defense and security budgets means the less there is to be spent on domestic programs. Or, for the purpose of this thesis, the more money spent on sports venue security, the less there is for other government expenditures. However, it is possible to add funding from other sources to push the curve outward in order to produce more guns and more butter.

266 "Guns and Butter Curve," *Investopedia.com,* accessed April 4, 2014.
http://www.investopedia.com/terms/g/gunsandbutter.asp.

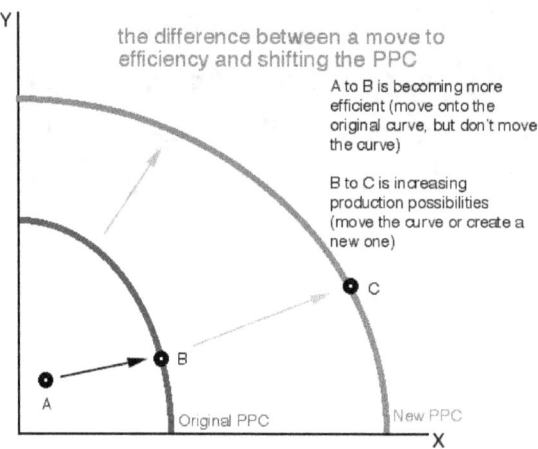

Figure 8.   Demonstrating an Improved Macro-Economic Model of Expenditure Returns[267]

As depicted in Figure 8, it is theoretically possible for additional funding to move the curve outward in order to facilitate production of both at a higher level. Therein lies a great political quandary continually waged between American parties as to how to generate the additional funds or resources to push the entire curve outward. In this thesis, the dilemma posed is how to recommend security enhancements that either (virtually) don't cost more money, or in the event they do, how to push the entire curve further outward by linking them to creative, new funding streams.

In answering Research Question 3 in the next section, several options will be addressed to meet the goal of enabling government to push the productivity curve outward without increasing the tax burden on the populace to an unacceptable level. However, to begin the cost-benefit analysis, scholars and public policy leaders should ask themselves: what is the minimum point of effectiveness to make the cost worth spending? Below is one brief example of what such a cost-benefit scenario might resemble.

> In the Boston public housing projects of Roxie Homes, Camfield Gardens, and Grant Manor, a major collaborative effort was recently undertaken to improve the quality of life. Trained security officers from the projects, who have arresting powers, monitor the CCTV camera from within the project and respond to any illegal activity captured on the video. The project, known as Safe Neighborhood Action Plan (SNAP), cost $1.3

---

[267] Narayan Bashyal, "Shifting the Production Possibility Curve," August 26, 2013, http://narayanbashyal75.blogspot.com/2013/08/economics-xi-hseb-notes.html.

million to implement and has reduced crime in the three projects by 30 percent.[268]

This demonstrates an example of cost of investment versus the successful return on that expenditure.

However, an example of the difficulty in weighing the cost-benefit is to consider the relationship of CCTVs with the resolution of the Boston Marathon Bombing. By a 2007 ACLU accounting, records show that in Boston there were an estimated 147 cameras in the networked city system and another 400 on subways and buses operated by the Massachusetts Bay Transportation Authority.[269] The attackers were subsequently identified because of the CCTVs in place at the event. The capture of the perpetrators within the week demonstrates the intrinsic value of surveillance technologies. An added benefit of the CCTV system in place, which was widely recognized by the media in the aftermath of the bombing, is the deterrent factor for future violence. Therefore, surveillance systems can provide a benefit in after-the-fact support to solve crime, a deterrent effect on future crime, and real-time help in interdiction to complete the venue protection mission.

This section will demonstrate a sufficiently high probability that the conclusions and recommended courses of action will achieve the goal of a "breakeven threshold" analysis. This means that a quantitative method will justify expenditures for surveillance or trace detection equipment (the known costs) included in certain more costly venue security options recommended in Chapter IV. The policy analysis decision framework used will enable uncertain factors to be addressed by comparing them with certain established costs. The end-state product is a decision model built from a response rule that says if the benefits exceed the costs, it is worth doing.[270] Mueller's cost-benefit analysis formula is one such academically recognized tool that will be used in this thesis.

---

[268] Marcus Nieto, Kimberly Johnston-Dodds and Charlene Wear Simmons, "Public and Private Applications of Video Surveillance," California Research Bureau, February 6, 2006, www.library.ca.gov/crb/02/06/02-006.pdf.

[269] Chenda Ngak, "Boston Marathon Investigation: Are CCTV Cameras the Answer?" *CBS News*, April 16, 2013, http://www.cbsnews.com/news/boston-marathon-investigation-are-cctv-cameras-the-answer.

[270] Eugene Bardach, *A Practical Guide for Policy Analysis: The Eightfold Path to More Effective Problem Solving.* 4th ed (Washington, DC: CQ Press, 2011), 50–53

2.   Costs, Breakeven Point, and Formula Applied

Mueller defines the benefit of a security measure as a function of three elements:

- Benefit = (probability of a successful attack)
- x (losses sustained in the successful attack)
- x (reduction in risk)

The "probability of a successful attack" is the estimated likelihood that a successful terrorist attack will take place if the security measure is not in place. The "losses sustained in the successful attack" include the fatalities and all direct and indirect damages that will accrue as a result of a successful terrorist attack. The "reduction in risk" is the degree to which the security measure is estimated to foil, deter, disrupt, or protect against a terrorist attack. This benefit, expressed as a multiplicative composite of the three considerations, is then compared to the costs of providing the security measure required to attain the benefit.[271] This means that if the cost to implement the measures is less than the benefit amount derived by the formula, then it is worth pursuing.

The factors used in this thesis are shown in Table 2:

One-time Damages	Subsequent Annual Damages
Value of Lives (Quantified by Mueller)	Subsequent Enhancements Instituted
Liability for Injuries	Ticket Sales
Facility Property Damage	Club Revenues Future Losses
Corollary Property (Adjacent Buildings)	Marketing Ad Losses
Response, Rescue, & Clean Up	Area Economic Disruption Activity
Reconstruction	Businesses Bankrupt as Result

Table 2.   Successful Attack Cost Factors[272]

[271] Mueller and Stewart, 76–77.

[272] Claude Journés, "Policing and Security: Terrorists and Hooligans." *Sport In Society* 1, no. 2 (1998): 145–60.

Therefore, to apply the formula it is necessary to approximate the losses sustained in a successful attack. This thesis will suggest the losses from multiple coordinated suicide bomb attacks with two delayed detonations occurring simultaneously at four geographically dispersed stadiums.

Using the value established in Mueller's 2011 text affixing $6.5 million per death, and using the Joint Improvised Explosive Device Defeat Organization (JIEDDO) bomb blast radius' at a crowded sporting venue, for demonstrating the formula the thesis will assume 15 deaths and 120 wounded in the dual bombings at each of the four venues, a total of 60 deaths and 480 wounded would result from the synchronized attack. This type of attack alone would yield losses of $390 million solely due to the deaths as quantified by Mueller. This may be a worst case scenario, but it is also not as extreme a scenario as could possibly be conjectured. The 1994 and 2010 World Cup viewing site attacks cited earlier in the chapter revealed virtually a 1:1 ratio of deaths to wounded victims. However, to use a less powerful attack as an example, if such an attack occurred due to one suicide bomber and resulted in only three deaths, (which for a densely populated venue would be extremely unlikely), then even by the Mueller attribution there would be $19.5 million in damages due to only the deaths involved. Adding to these formulaic projections, the other categories cited above would dramatically increase the potential quantitative value of the damages from such attacks.

Therefore, reverting to the Mueller formula:

If asserting a 95% chance of success for coordinated multiple suicide bomb attacks at various SEAR 4 MLB venues, along with a $390M quantitative damage assessment solely from the deaths incurred, then multiplying this amount against an asserted security enhancement estimate will yield a Benefit. In this example, a 75% chance is asserted that a given HSE measure can reduce the likelihood of the attack's success

With this data the formula would reveal:

Benefit = .95 x 390,000,000 x .75 = $277,875,000

This means that if the HSE were to implement measures that could produce a 75% reduction in likelihood of an attack's success, then it is advisable to spend up to $277.8 million to implement the measures. Of course, this is just one possible example. If in our same example using only 60 deaths but the projected likelihood of success before the measure is implemented and the effectiveness of the measure stopping the attack are respectively reduced, then the formula might appear as:

Benefit = .50 x 390,000,000 x .50 = $97,500,000

This figure now resembles one that can be considered much more palatable by the collaborative public-private sector, especially if spread out over a number of years.

In considering surveillance equipment costs, during the installation the cost of the cameras is not the most expensive factor. Rather, the more expensive elements are the installation, maintenance, inter-operability of the systems, training and operations center staffing, according to BWI Airport security system invoicing.[273] Infrastructure cost for the facility can include opportunity costs for lost retail/revenue generating space. In addition to that opportunity cost, maintenance, and eventual technology upgrade constitute recurring expenses. In the long term, the highest cost consideration is for increases in staff to accommodate SOC or system monitoring schedules, as this will be a routine annual expense.

However, to consider calculating solely the costs of select types of surveillance and trace detection systems (i.e., just the camera system and ETD system hardware) to improve venue security, for demonstration purposes, the CPI adjusted figures are estimated as shown in Table 3.[274]

---

[273] Determined from Baltimore Washington International (BWI) ADT invoicing data.

[274] Surveillance and Trace Detection equipment costs have been established in 2014 dollars based on Bureau of Labor, Consumer Price Indexed totals from data acquired by TSA and as posted by technology providing companies. Prices are per system as an approximation for demonstration purposes.

CCTV	$13,118
Facial Recognition CCTV	$25k for first camera system plus $10k for each additional camera
ETD	$60,325

Table 3.   Surveillance and Detection Equipment Costs[275]

For example, it is reasonable to presume that $200,000 could procure an ETD system and 11 integrated CCTVs for synchronization into a SOC. This may not sound like an extensive system but for a SEAR 5 Minor League Baseball facility that only has one main turnstile entrance, as is the case at the Prince George's Stadium sited earlier in the chapter, then it can be a profoundly effective addition to the security team's resources. From these figures, and from a further analysis of the myriad of varying stadium sizes and configurations, purposes, and locations, it is clear that the costs to implement surveillance and detection technologies for a SEAR 5 MiLB or NCAA sporting venue will be less expensive than for a SEAR 4 MLB, NFL, or select NCAA venue.

As an alternative cost-benefit scenario for consideration, the figures below illustrate the option of taking no action to support SEAR 4 and 5 venues in upgrading their security capabilities, and subsequently a lethal coordinated attack does occur. In such a case, as with aviation industry security in 2001, the HSE may find itself in the same predicament as it was following the al Qaeda attacks. Responding to massive public opinion and deep fear, developing an after-the-fact type of "knee-jerk" defensive strategy can also be approximated.

In 2004, TSA analyzed expenditures incurred to implement heightened or enhanced security measures at the nation's largest airports directly as a result of the 2001 attacks (i.e., these expenses were not in place prior to the attacks). An example of the study's results as shown in Table 4 revealed that at the Phoenix Sky Harbor International airport, annual costs increased.

---

[275] "Surveillance System Pricing Sheet," SecurLinx, accessed February 1, 2014, http://www.securlinx.com/BR/pdf_files/FaceTrac%20Data%20Sheet.pdf. The $12,000 per camera installed price with training, Bureau of Labor CPI adjusted 1.5% a year since 2008. This denotes the approximate average of the purchase of fixed and "PTZ" cameras. PTZ cameras are "Point, Tilt, Zoom" cameras. BWI uses the fixed cameras at stairwells, elevators, doorways. The PTZs are for larger areas to watch people, to pick up on behavior or an individual and to monitor them as necessary; $50,000-per-ETD system installed price with training, Bureau of Labor CPI adjusted 2.11% a year since 2005

Personnel	$2.7M/yr
Equipment	$950k/yr
Facility Infrastructure	$1.05M/yr
Operations/Procedures	$650k/yr
Total	$5.26M/yr
Total CPI Adjusted to 2014	$6.55M/yr

Table 4.   9/11 Aftermath Increased Security Costs[276]

This airport handles a throughput of approximately 110,000 passengers per day. So to pro-rate that throughput number to one comparable for an average daily throughput of patrons at an MLB SEAR 4 event, of 30,000 attendees per game per day, the thesis will use a 27% size pro-ration. Therefore, if similar costs used by TSA to adjust airports to a heightened threat after a catastrophic attack were to be implemented then costs may be proportioned for a SEAR 4 venue to expect possible costs of 27% or .27 x $6.55M = $1.77M.[277]   This approximation would cover costs for personnel, equipment, facility infrastructure, and operations/procedures to attain a higher level of security at SEAR 4–5 venues comparable to the checkpoint and surveillance systems at today's airports.

The data in this section is used to demonstrate the breadth of the costs to consider for strengthening SEAR 4–5 venue security. Further discussion of the arguments, on both sides of the spending spectrum, are addressed in more detail below.

3.   Considerations and Contentions against Increased Expenditures

This section addresses the expenditures that should be considered to add enhanced surveillance and trace detection equipment to SEAR 4–5 venues.

One important argument against increased HSE expenditures raises the question, is there "a false sense of insecurity in the United States?"[278]   Data reflect that since 9/11

---

[276]Airports Council International—North America, "2004 Survey: The Cost of Security since 9/11."

[277] These figures were attained in 2004. Therefore, using the CPI adjusted rate of 2.22% per year, this means that an expenditure per stadium of $1.77M annually would equate to similar security measures for a facility with a pro-rated throughput, to reflect that of the MLB SEAR 4 venues. Bureau of Labor, Consumer Price Index, http://www.in2013dollars.com/2003-dollars-in-2013?amount=100, retrieved 3/1/14

[278] Attributed to Leif Wenar of the University of Sheffield, as cited by John Mueller in "Six Rather Unusual Propositions,"487.

there have been only 27 deaths as a result of terrorist attack. Notwithstanding the 297 wounded or injured in such attacks here in America, critics opposing expanded HS budgets have cited that the media does not seem to inform the public that "in every year except 2001 only a few hundred people in the entire world have died as a result of international terrorism."[279]

Perhaps it is needless to state, but if you are one of the "only a few hundred" that have died, terrorism was a critically important issue to you and the families and friends you left behind. Accordingly, for the governments representing those few hundred people, it is implicit in the role of government to make public safety and security a primary, if not singularly most important reason for existence as a sovereign government, i.e., to protect the people from all enemies, foreign and domestic.[280] The gravest disservice the government can do for its people is to not even attempt to find means to provide better, even idealist, solutions just because of the notion they may involve cost.

Another argument against expenditures for surveillance and detection equipment contends that enhancing venue security technologies and staff training may lead to the government failing to spend money on other ventures perhaps "of objectively greater societal needs."[281] Whether or not any single government expenditure is truly of an "objectively greater need" by any sense of measurable standard certainly is subject to political debate. But the point remains that CT defensive posture spending on Homeland Security means that funds allocated there could arguably be spent better elsewhere, e.g., addressing poverty, joblessness, or climate change.

A similar argument contends that Americans suffer when the domestic agenda does not continue to obtain endless funding, and that deviating from this principle weakens the nation's economic engine. By virtue of the government pursuing

---

[279] Mueller, "Six Rather Unusual Propositions," 487.

[280] "Oaths of Office," U.S. Army, accessed on February 21, 2014, http://www.history.army.mil/html/faq/oaths.html.

[281] Clark Chapman and Alan W. Harris, "A Skeptical Look at September 11th." *Skeptical Inquirer* 26, no. 5 (2002): 30; Mueller and Stewart, *Terror, Security, and Money*, XX.

"unachievable but politically popular levels of domestic security," the terrorists achieve one of their goals, for the U.S. to damage its long-term financial future.[282]

A more questionable argument asserts that building a strong "homeland security industry" is only in the best interest of the few that can profit from it. This point infers that the homeland security industry is profiting from hyped fear mongering about terrorism purported by pundits who fabricate and perpetuate the culture of fear. The theory contends that the conjured insecurity in America is the result of media frenzy created by news channels and expert panels that encourage viewers to watch their programming and their commercials.[283] This promoted insecurity also infers a highly motivated private sector with foundations in the military weapons and homeland security technologies industries driven by profit.[284] It is also reasoned that this homeland security industry may yield not only corporate profits for those producing equipment and technologies but also benefits the public officials who sell trust through security to their constituents.[285] And finally it is hypothesized that the over-reaction to increase HSE expenditures could be just a knee-jerk reaction of insecurity by a people that have been largely geographically isolated from enemies for centuries and now find themselves immersed in a global village and unnecessarily afraid that danger lurks in the heart of every foreigner.

Essentially, the sum of these arguments asks if there is any basis for "housewives in Iowa ... to be watching TV afraid that al-Qaeda's going to charge in their front door?"[286]

Nonetheless, as the answer to Research Question 1 demonstrates, there is a viable terrorist threat that is capable and willing to strike soft targets to kill American non-combatants. Obviously, organizers and promoters of SEAR 4–5 rated sporting events cannot afford security expenditures on the scale of nations preparing to host an Olympics

---

282 Mueller, "Six Rather Unusual Propositions," 492.

283 Ibid., 492–493

284 Ibid.

285 Ibid., 493, 495.

286 Mark Bowden's remarks on PBS's *Tucker Carlson: Unfiltered,* which aired November 19, 2004.

or FIFA World Cup competition. But if they could cost-effectively structure the same security measures on a pro-rated scale commensurate with the size and visibility of their event in comparison to those fortified mega-events, would they? If there was no adverse cost attached and they could even use the venue security to promote the events, using it as a marketing tool to their business advantage, would they?

Similar to the U.K., as cited in chapter two, the U.S. government is essentially responsible for the security from the stadium property outward into society, and ostensibly the private sector is responsible for the security from the stadium property inward to the playing surface at the venue.[287] Accordingly, with the private sector bearing the bulk of the responsibility for security on location, there is a need for incentive, or necessity,[288] for it to continually improve the last line of security on-site. The law enforcement community suggested that, especially with smaller (SEAR 4–5) venues, the city and county governments should consider policies or legislation to require more direct cooperation between the private sector venue managers and the authorities.[289] The incentive and requisite- based options should not be ruled out for future consideration, and will be further addressed in this thesis.

Short of the more sweeping mandatory parameter, other incentive-based options have been attempted. To enhance venue safety and to facilitate better risk management, private sector companies in the United States are financially incentivized in the form of insurance cost reductions to obtain more suitable facilities and better prepared venue staff. However, there is no evidence that these insurance rate reductions are reserved for Counterterrorism (CT) strategy.

Instead, they are incentives for property managers to ensure safety precautions and emergency procedures are in place. This raises the substantial point that there is a fine, yet important distinction, between venue safety programs and facility-event CT

---

[287] International Association of Chiefs of Police (IACP), Community Oriented Policing Services (COPS), *Building Private Security/Public Policing Partnerships to Prevent and Respond to Terrorism and Disorder* (Washington, DC: U.S. Department of Justice, 2004), 23–24, http://www.cops.usdoj.gov/mime/open.pdf?Item=1355.

[288] Ibid.

[289] Ibid., 24

strategy. It is possible that property managers obtain the insurance cost reduction incentive simply by ensuring that crowd control measures and first responder measures are in place. However, there is no direct link attributing cost incentives with the installation and maintenance of enhanced counterterrorist surveillance and detection systems to improve attendee safety by thwarting terrorist attacks.

But what of the cost-benefit analysis offered by opponents to increased spending? If the cost of the security measure is $1 more than the benefit attained, does this define the measure as unworthy of implementation? What is the margin of error in the accuracy of the study data presented by either side of this argument? The cost figures are so immense and oftentimes so immeasurable that any cost-benefit analysis performed must be acknowledged to have an alarmingly high level of subjectivity or inaccuracy.

A further contention regarding cost-benefit arguments rests in the qualitative factors previously stated. What is the obligation and responsibility of government to protect all citizens, not just those that are cost-effective to protect? What is the obligation to protect the people as a fundamental pillar for the right to govern? These may be rhetorical questions because their answers rest in the intrinsic nature of government, rendering it impossible to assert a quantitative value. Finally, there is the intangible factor of the value of security itself, i.e., for the peace of mind for the people over whom the government governs.

These questions clearly constitute a more extensive level of effort is needed to fully account for a cost-benefit analysis than this thesis will be able to endeavor. This raises the daunting specter for scholars and public policy practitioners that perhaps national defense and homeland security are too complex to adjudicate cost effectiveness based solely on quantifiable data. Because there is no easy way to fully account for intrinsically intangible factors, such as the value of peace, the non-loss of life, or the capability to protect. It is also challenging to equitably compare the cost of a security strategy employed against its own success when the latter is predicated on an absence of death, destruction, or damages.

4. Federal Funding Sources: FEMA Grants and Government Expenditures in Comparison

When studying potential resources to support select security enhancements to SEAR 4–5 venues, FEMA is a chief consideration due to its designation by DHS as the largest funding source to support the achievement of the core capabilities described in the National Planning Framework. For federal grants and distributions to the state, local, and NGO stakeholders, FEMA possessed a budget of $6 billion in FY 12.[290] In 2013, FEMA was authorized to issue $558.7 million under the State Homeland Security Program (SHSP), and an additional $354.6 Million under the Urban Area Security Initiative (UASI). Both of these programs are part of the Homeland Security Grant Program (HSGP).

A similar federal grant program that can serve as a model for SEAR 4–5 security funding is already in existence within TSA. The Transit Security Grant Program (TSGP) is intended "to strengthen the Nation's critical infrastructure against risks associated with potential terrorist attacks."[291] The TSGP provides funds to transit system owner/operators for strengthening their security against terrorism, thereby demonstrating existing precedent for such a possible sports venue funding model.

The HSGP plays a vital role in the annual implementation of the National Preparedness System (NPS) by supporting the building, sustainment, and delivery of the core capabilities addressed earlier in this chapter. The HSGP aims to support the attaining of the National Preparedness Goal (NPG) of a secure and resilient nation. As discussed previously, achieving the core capabilities are not the responsibility of any single level of government, organization, or community, but rather, it requires the "whole of community" concept described in the PPD and National Planning Framework. The FY

---

[290]U.S. Department of Homeland Security (DHS). DHS Financial Assistance, accessed April, 2, 2014, http://www.dhs.gov/dhs-financial-assistance. http://www.dhs.gov/dhs-financial-assistance.

[291] U.S. Transportation Security Administration (TSA), "Transit Security Grant Program," March 31, 2014, http://www.tsa.gov/stakeholders/transit-security-grant-program-4.

2013 HSGP supports core capabilities across the five mission areas of Prevention, Protection, Mitigation, Response, and Recovery based on allowable costs.[292]

As an example of the capability of DHS to allocate funds for sporting venue security, it provided a grant for $568,000 to the University of Southern Mississippi to study vulnerability and risks at collegiate sporting venues in 2005. This is just one example that precedent exists for DHS expenditure in the field. This manner of grant spending or budget allocation is in keeping with the purpose of the protection mission. Of course, when approaching the debate over whether government funding is worthwhile to be spent on innovative homeland security concepts, it is beneficial to consider some other examples of domestic spending that have been highly recognized for their wastefulness or frivolous connections to productive domestic spending. If it is a matter of creating the small budget necessary to improve security at America's sporting venues, then many examples of programs could be examined in the light of further scrutiny to determine their worthiness to make room for security spending.

There are numerous watchdog reports on the merit, or waste, of various government expenditures. It is acknowledged that some may be debatable as to intrinsic value to the people, but presented here are just a few examples only to demonstrate that streamlining fiscal expenditures can free up funds for security programs. In 2009 it was revealed that the Defense Department wasted $100 million on unused flight tickets and failed to collect refunds even though the tickets were refundable.[293]   Despite trillion-dollar deficits, the 2009 approved U.S. federal budget contained 10,160 earmarks including one for $200,000 for a tattoo removal program in Mission Hills, California; $190,000 for the Buffalo Bill Historical Center in Cody, Wyoming; and $75,000 for the

---

[292] To further emphasize the effect government funding and legislation will have on video surveillance spending, IMS Research noted that the U.S. Federal Emergency Management Agency (FEMA) has issued 11 grants for physical security equipment and video surveillance that have generated millions of dollars of spending in the industry; "Research Firm Expects Bombings in Boston to Spur CCTV Spending," *Security Sales & Integration*, April 29, 2013. http://www.securitysales.com/article/research-firm-expects-bombings-in-boston-to-spur-cctv-spending/Boston_Marathon_Bombings

[293] Brian Reidl, *50 Examples of Government Waste* (Washington, DC: The Heritage Foundation. October 6, 2009), http://www.heritage.org/research/reports/2009/10/50-examples-of-government-waste#_edn45.

Totally Teen Zone in Albany, Georgia.[294] GAO discovered that more than one third of the 2.5 million recipients of emergency assistance following Hurricane Katrina committed fraud in applying for or spending assistance monies, accounting for $2 billion, including for the payment of a sex change operation. As a last example, related to sports, the 2012 Super Bowl Champion Baltimore Ravens were paid $130,000 in taxpayer money to promote the Affordable Care Act.

These are not raised as alarmist examples of scandal sheet media, but rather to point out that the adage of "where there's a will, there's a way" applies to government. If it is understood and accepted that there is a sector of the U.S. public that is vulnerable to a terrorist attack and proactive measures can be taken to prevent harm (even if it costs a modicum of federal funds), then the government owes it to the American people to at the very least examine these viable and invaluable possibilities.

The purpose of this Research Question is to examine an objective means of weighing a cost-benefit analysis in order to respond to opposition of new forms of HSE expenditure. The analysis has demonstrated that there are quantifiable methods to adjudicate and deem select expenditures as worthy and pragmatic. Further, this section has revealed that the sports entertainment sector may be one of the very few business sectors in America that can be teamed with the private sector as well as with resource input from the patrons to share in the costs. There exist current models of government-private sector cooperation that also include the customer-citizens to establish forms of "voluntary taxes," or funding for government coordinated projects. For example, the U.K. has set up the Football Foundation, and within the U.S., the TSA serves as such a model. These models and more policy options will be examined in the analysis answering Research Question 3.

---

294 Reidl, *50 Examples of Government Waste*.

D. RESEARCH QUESTION 3

If evolution in security for SEAR 4–5 events is needed, what cost-effective public policy action or solutions can be synthesized into a new Counter-Terrorism protection paradigm?

If we work together, we're stronger than if we work separately. Folks in the sports industry have been willing and helpful participants in this notion of shared responsibility.[295]

—Janet Napolitano,
Secretary of Homeland Security

This final section of the Analysis chapter will consider innovative public policy proposals to be considered in order to provide enhanced security at SEAR 4–5 venues. These options will be categorized, essentially, into those that are not costly, and those that may be costly but addressed through creative collaborative funding efforts.

Initially, this thesis has not advocated for the fortification of every semblance of infrastructure (i.e., to allocate resources to protect everything, everywhere, always). That, of course, would be impractical if not impossible.[296] However, the sports entertainment industry is one, like the aviation industry, that is very suitable for striking a public-private sector collaboration to include voluntary participation by the consumers to meet the costs of advisable fiscal expenditures.

Before examining such options, it is necessary to review certain relevant legal issues which have either been addressed or still need to be addressed. These precedents and issues will have an impact on what public policy options can be considered now, and which may need to be re-visited in the future.

One key issue revealed in the literature was that the legal responsibility of venue security is borne by facility owners and operators. The review also discovered that merely an understanding of legal obligations is insufficient and that venue managers must act on

---

[295] Bill Carey, "Stadium Security Continues to Evolve 10 Years After 9/11," *SI.com*, September 9, 2001, http://sportsillustrated.cnn.com/2011/more/09/06/stadium.security.changes.since.9.11/.

[296] Mueller, "Six Propositions about Terrorism," 493.

their duty of care, proactively taking measures to meet their obligations to ensure the security of their patrons to the best of their ability.

It has been a longstanding view that many citizens have been willing to trade privacy for safety, and thus did not mind "being watched."[297]   Though controversial when first revealed, the Edward Snowden leak of government surveillance practices in 2013 affirmed that most Americans are eager to know of the government practices, but yet still believe the practices are more helpful to catch terrorists than they are harmful to privacy interests.[298]

However, looking into the future to establish maximum use of surveillance systems with stored databases raises several legal challenges. Commissioned by the E.U., Schütz, et al., posited a scenario where databases and CCTV monitoring can be combined with facial recognition cameras to identify and recognize members of various terrorist or criminal offender databases. The concept of using the most advanced research to develop ever-improving surveillance equipment appears to be tremendously advantageous to the HSE. Specifically, the futuristic scenario includes:

> Increasingly transcending into cyberspace, following traces of when-, where- and whatever the user intends to do. That way a finely nuanced profiling of (potential) perpetrators of violence at the Football World Cup can take place. Security service providers do not only have access to police databases with a variety of information on criminal offenders, they also cooperate with large private IT companies in order to create profiles of people who could attract attention through violent behaviour during the World Cup. In order to discover, for example, hooligans who do not already have a criminal record, Internet forums of fan communities and social networks are systematically scanned and automatically analysed. Raising an alarm and creating a preliminary blacklist, the fully automated analysis does not only consist of a search of keywords but draws on new semantic web technologies that are able to put words into the correct context and gain the relevant information out of billions of entries.[299]

---

[297] Jennifer M. Granholm, "Video Surveillance on Public Streets: The Constitutionality of Invisible Citizen Searches," *University of Detroit Law Review* 4, no. 64 (1987): 687–713.

[298] Dana Blanton, "Fox News Poll: Most Voters Glad They Know Snowden Secrets." *Fox News*, January 22, 2014, http://www.foxnews.com/politics/2014/01/22/fox-news-poll-most-voters-glad-know-snowden-secrets/.

[299] Schütz et al., *Smart Surveillance, 3.*

The intent of such a futuristic vision is to enable a government to assemble files on individuals (e.g., that now merit presence on the TSA No Fly List or are Known or Suspected Terrorists [KST]). In this scenario, the government can include pictures so that facial recognition-smart cameras can be alerted to their presence in crowds. On-site security teams or local LE can then provide surveillance on the identified KSTs, or apprehend them immediately.

However, in America, this future scenario raises several unanswered questions. Because SEAR 4–5 venue security teams are almost exclusively private sector employees, how can a Top Secret classified database be shared with them? Even if the database itself is not revealed to the private sector employees, individuals will be revealed to be in the database each time such a surveillance recognition system alerts the private sector security team member to the presence of the KST.

Further, even if such a government classified information issue could be resolved to enable the database to be used for identity recognition purposes by a private sector employee, or even by a government employee stationed in the SOC, an operational issue arises. Specifically, if the person identified by the technology is already in a KST database, then there is a distinct possibility that if that person somehow managed to gain entry to the U.S., or is a home-grown radical, there may be a federal operation on-going that is currently monitoring the individual. Or, conceivably, the government may be working with him/her in a collaborative operation for national security interests. This complex scenario means that if the SEAR 4–5 security team at the SOC on location finds this individual matching up, then what? Do they move forward with surveillance or apprehension of the individual when it is very possible that it may destroy an operational plan already in action by another government agency?

Finally, the legal question is raised regarding liability issues in the event of a false positive, i.e., the surveillance system identifies an individual in the crowd as a member of the KST database, but upon apprehension, it turns out that the system erred. There would be a myriad of grounds on which damages could possibly be proven to exploit the government's vulnerability. The government may then be susceptible to paying not only monetary damages, but incurring great criticism and mistrust from the people, the media, and Congress. Another potentially troubling aspect of the false positive scenario is the possibility of damaging an ongoing operation by means of "tipping off" KSTs that the government wrongly assailed a citizen that bore a resemblance to a particular terrorist.

Therefore, though facial recognition CCTV has greatly advanced over the course of the past decade, for use at sporting event venues as a protective security resource it still is a technology in need of more technical fine tuning and a great deal of resolution in legal forums.

1. Cost-Effective Options with Little or No Cost: Improving Doctrine, Training, and Compliance

In lieu of leadership choosing to pursue options that may bear some expense, there are alternative options that are not costly. These options pertain to doctrine and training.

The first inexpensive option is to push for the completion and production of the National Protection Framework without any further delays. In 2011, the President required DHS to produce the National Planning Framework. Well into his second term and three years later, only four of the five component parts have been published, awaiting the National Protection Framework portion to be completed and approved for release

Related to this, if the published version of the National Protection Framework is akin to the Working Draft, it has ample room for notably more specificity. It is acknowledged that the Core Capabilities strategy is to enable the state/local stakeholders to have a great amount of responsibility for tailoring doctrine to suit their needs. However, the Protection Framework as drafted does not spell out any specific standards that can be measured uniformly across the national spectrum. Inevitably, this will predictably result in disparities in regions and localities as to the types of practices that are performed, or not. Regional differences will not allow for the obtaining of standardized measurements, and this fact will reduce the significance of the NPF as a whole. Therefore, at this time, it is possible that DHS can re-work the NPF to include tangible goals, milestones, and metrics so that useful information will be obtained in the future to best meet the objectives/goals of the NPF.

Perhaps not only can Frameworks be produced for each PPD outlined Mission, but within each Framework there can be Annexes derived broken down to address specific aspects within the broad context of the National Protection Framework. This measure is not intended to be heavy-handed or needlessly instruct the state/local stakeholders on how to structure their procedures, but rather to ensure that security teams across the nation all use the same playbook, so to speak. As explained in Chapter II, the U.K. national government provides training and a dedicated resource to the police department level to directly assist with the specific mission of sporting event local policing.

However, even with implementation, research has shown that complacency and local resource constraints are substantial enemies to the HSE. With only Best Practices suggested for consideration, and no ostensible means to inspect or confirm the execution of these recommendations, there is effectively no operational procedure in place. Even if the over-arching strategy of this Administration is to enable the state/local stakeholders to determine what is best for them regarding tactics on location, it is naive to assume that 100% of facility managers will have either the incentive or resources to implement suggested practices.

One low-cost solution to the inspection and compliance void is the establishment of a small office within DHS to synchronize with Fusion Centers and the Offices of the Federal Coordinators in the respective states. This office would determine and verify inspection dates and compliance deadlines. As a brief example of the scope of funding to support such an office within DHS, in 2005, DHS granted $568,000 to study the security vulnerabilities in collegiate sporting venues. Likely only half of this amount could support an office of three personnel within DHS annually to accomplish the dedicated mission of inspection and compliance with viable milestones and metrics established for the facility managers nationwide.

Other organizational options could be considered as well. The U.K. has demonstrated impressive success at addressing its domestic criminal concern of hooliganism with a top-down organizational system designed to support local policing strategies. The scale of the national policing doctrine in the U.K., which operates 52 police departments, is much smaller and more manageable than in the U.S., which

95

operates more than 1700 police departments. Nevertheless, the organizational structure has proved effective in the U.K.'s local policing operations and could be adapted to the scale of the U.S.

To elaborate, the U.K. dedicates Football Liaison (FLO) and Football Intelligence Officers (FIO) to the local police department level. Among other duties, the FLO audits the safety measures provided by the sporting club/team through attendance and observation at events. The FIO coordinates with other local law enforcement agencies and recognized team supporter groups, as well as coordinates intelligence gathering prior to and during events. These are examples of direct support from the national level that greatly support the front-line level coordination and standard consistency across the nation.

The U.S. counterterrorism strategy is reliant on local policing to detect, disrupt, and interdict terrorism before or during the unfolding of such plans in our midst. The insertion of a DHS liaison to the state and local level in order to have eyes on the ground and direct connection to the numerous federal agencies and resources would serve several tangible purposes. Operationally, much like the FIOs at the local level in the U.K., it would mean an active full-time presence dedicated to the daily protection mission as it applies to the sports and entertainment industry, an important American business sector. Strategically it would signify a presence with whom the facility managers would interact in a collaborative manner to assist with meeting milestones and metrics. This active partnership would help eliminate complacency for practice implementation while providing another conduit for access and support in acquiring supplemental resources to facilitate improvements and inspection compliance.

Another successful procedural model employed in the U.K. is the issuance of an annual "Safety Certificate" upon the verification of staff training standards.[300] The Safety Certificates are issued by the Football Licensing Authority (FLA). The FLA was statutorily established by the national government to ensure all spectators "are able to

---

[300] ACPO, *Guidance on Policing Football*, 24.

attend sports stadia in safety, comfort, and security."[301] There currently is no such equivalent in the U.S.

Although the U.K. model is inclusive of crowd management, control, and general safety, such training standards in the U.S. can be adapted for terrorism response and first-responder operational partnership support and exercises. The planning and execution of such inspected training can simultaneously provide an incentive and requirement to the private sector venue managers. While these viable courses of action ostensibly have little or no price tag to increase the national debt or require pilfering from the domestic agenda budget, there also exist monetary options worth consideration. These monetary options could be coupled with innovative funding strategies in order to yield little expense to the government.

2.   Solutions with Some Expense Coupled with Innovative Funding

As was demonstrated in the research and analysis of Chapters II and III, there are evolving and advancing technologies which become more attainable as time passes. PTZ CCTV systems have continued to shrink in price over the past decade and some versions of monitoring software are now offered online for free. American CCTV industry sales figures depict a steady upward trend for residential and commercial use. CCTV usage has become so commonplace in the U.K. that there are now more cameras in use (5.9 million) than there are people living in the neighboring nation of Scotland (5.3 million).[302] The takeaway from rapidly advancing CCTV technology, tied to decreasing costs, is that it is possible for sporting venue facilities and parking lots of any size to be observed by CCTVs and linked in to local SOCs.

Since its inaugural contracts with DHS in 2006 the price of the Z-Portal automobile X-ray system is decreasing in time, and its success has led cost-conscious institutions and nations around the world to purchase this system.[303] Though perhaps

---

[301] Ibid.

[302] "Scotland's Population at its Highest Ever," National Records of Scotland, August 8, 2013, http://www.nrscotland.gov.uk/news/2013/scotlands-population-at-its-highest-ever.

[303] American Science & Engineering (AS&E). "American Science and Engineering, Inc. Receives $4.5 Million Order for Z Portal and Gemini X-ray Systems to Secure Checkpoints at Middle Eastern University," news release, October 1, 2013. http://ir.as-e.com/releasedetail.cfm?releaseid=794210.

initially perceived by critics as an expensive luxury security item, subsequent supplemental purchases by DHS in recent years have validated its worth in security practice at CBP, qualifying it as a suitable protection mission resource for many venue parking facilities.[304] Similarly, though Explosive Trace Detection (ETD) systems have been generally unsuited for application to sizeable crowds pouring through limited turnstile entrances at sporting venues, the PHASE (photo-acoustic) ETD systems may soon be on the market. Such a breakthrough, which has been achieved technologically and awaits the product availability for purchase, should astutely be worked into acquisitions and doctrinal operations plans now.

However, achieving an upgrade to surveillance and detection equipment at SEAR 4–5 event venues could prove expensive. This reality combined with the circumstance that many of the facilities are fiscally constrained in a profit-driven market economy, means that it may be necessary to find ways to provide funding for equipment acquisition and training. Acknowledging this dilemma, however, does not mean that the federal government should immediately dismiss the simplest of considerations as to how it might be possible to obtain them or require them to be deployed. Just because the acquisition and deployment plan may be challenging, or even require an outlay of funding, there are collaborative options worth considering that will be to the collective benefit of all.

For the purchase of CCTV, ETD, and Auto X-ray systems the government could seek and build a partnership with the private sector and with the patrons attending the events to generate revenues to cover system implementations and upgrades. This would not be the first time such a collaborative funding effort was achieved.

In the aftermath of the 9/11 attacks, the TSA was created. As a measure to help offset its aviation security expenses, the "Security Fee" was added to the airline ticket price. The fee was intended to avert an influx of national debt and increased taxation by putting the onus of the burden for funding on the citizens that use the aviation industry,

---

[304] "U.S. CBP Places $19.3 Million Follow-on Order for AS&E's Z Backscatter Vans ZBVs." Port Technology International, October 21, 2009, http://www.porttechnology.org/news/us_cbp_places_193_million_follow_on_order_for_ases_z_backscatter_vans_zbvs; "Defense Daily, An Access Intelligence, LLC Service," *Defense Daily*, May 23, 2012, http://www.defensedaily.com/Assets/File/txt/TR2_2012-05-22_14-31.txt.

and thereby, its security system. In a statutorily innovative move, a sort of voluntary tax was implemented. The original TSA Security Fee launched in 2002, established a $2.50 per leg of trip fee, with a $5 maximum fee per one way trip.[305] That maximum one-way trip fee would now be a Consumer Price Indexed value of $3.79 in comparison to 2002 dollars.[306] There is no evidence that this nominal security fee has adversely affected airline ticket sales. Illustrated in Figure 9 are the FY13 figures denoting aviation security expenses and fee revenues collected from passengers and airlines to offset the costs.

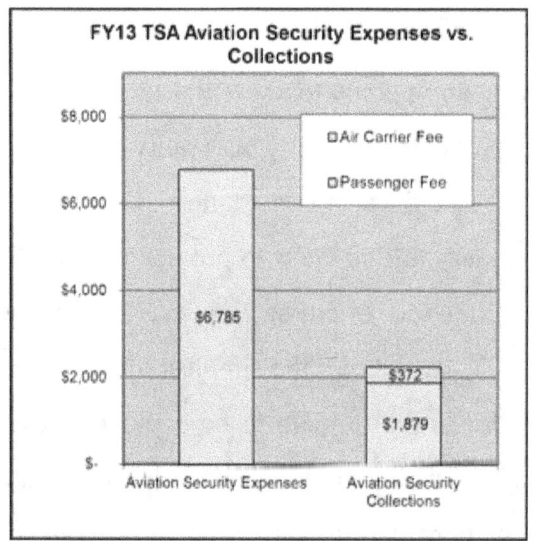

Figure 9.   Aviation Security Expenses vs. Aviation Fee Collections FY13[307]

To summarize (Monetary figures rounded to the tenth of $billion):

- FY13 total aviation security expenses were $6.8 billion;

- FY13 total aviation security fee collections were $2.3 billion;

- $1.9 billion in aviation security expenses (28%) funded through air traveler security fees;

- $372 million in aviation security expenses (5%) funded through air carrier security fees;

---

[305] 49 U.S. Code § 44940 - Security Service Fee.

[306] "$5 in 2014 → $3.79 in 2002," In2013Dollars.com, accessed April 2, 2014, http://www.in2013dollars.com/2014-dollars-in-2002?amount=5.

[307] Transportation Security Administration, Office of Revenue, "Transportation Security Fees," December, 2014, 2. http://www.tsa.gov/stakeholders/historical-fee-collection-data

- $4.5 billion in aviation security expenses (67%) funded through federal budget appropriations.

Following the implementation in 2002, the Aviation Security fee revenues grew with the returning success of the airline travel industry. Since 2005, the fee revenues have remained very consistent, averaging $1.9 billion annually, within a 2% +/- window each year.[308] The airline travel industry is cited as an example here because with 376 million fee generating tickets sold, it is similar in scale to the sports entertainment industry, with 256 million potentially fee generating tickets sold among the seven major American sports in 2013.[309] Therefore, the TSA Security Fee model is a solid example of the potential volume and benefit that a voluntary user tax that can serve the sports entertainment industry.

Because the sports entertainment industry is one of the few in the American economy that is similar in size and scope to the travel industry, it is a potential large pool of untapped financial resources. As demonstrated in the model above, the Aviation Security Fee is not intended to cover the entire amount of the TSA security expense. Rather, it is intended to help offset the security costs. However, adding a similar security fee to the ticket price for SEAR 4–5 venues would not require the establishment of the vast institutional headquarters that was necessary to stand-up TSA and maintain agency operations. Therefore, with only the need for a limited office to manage such a DHS program, a tremendously larger percentage of the revenues generated can be put directly toward facility security equipment, personnel security training upgrades, and inspection and compliance practices.

Regarding patron open-mindedness toward understanding and accepting such a security fee, currently many sporting event ticket offices include a "Convenience Fee" at least as expensive as the TSA Security fee cited above.[310] Such a convenience fee is added to the price of a ticket solely for private-sector revenue, having no apparent

---

[308] Ibid., 3.

[309] Includes attendance totals for MLB, MiLB, NFL, NHL, NBA, MLS, and NCAA Football and Basketball.

[310] Orioles.com asserts a $6 convenience fee on each ticket purchased online.

purpose for the public benefit. Thus, it is possible that in the sports and entertainment industry, such a publicly beneficial security fee will be not perceived as an issue of much concern for the majority of patrons. It is extremely unlikely to adversely affect attendance figures for club owners and NCAA institutions any more than such already established and culturally accepted "convenience fees."

Even if there was some remote possibility that a proportionally small fee would influence patrons and ticket sales, there is the very possible, if not likely, consideration to tier the fee according to price-range of the events and the tickets sold within the event. Of course, this may raise questions from select groups concerning a perceived imposed tax. However, few activist organizations have successfully argued with the long-standing precedents of higher fees and taxes levied on those that are proven more able to afford it. In the event of opposition to this fee, one option to address the opposition could be a tiered approach to assessing the fee. For example, the fee attached to ticket sales for venues seating less than 5,000 patrons would be minimal. The security fee would then slightly escalate as the venue sizes increase (e.g., from 5–20,000, 20–55,000, 55,000 and above). This would in essence reflect the general ticket pricing for local, small college events, then progressing through the larger college/smaller professional events to the largest college/professional football venues. Further, within the seating categories, the fee could be slightly higher for Club level and Luxury Suite seats than for the lowest priced seats located in the rafters of a given building or amid the clouds of a given stadium.

As an example, in Baltimore's Camden Yards baseball park, as is the case with virtually all professional club sporting stadiums and arenas, luxury suites and club level tickets are for premium seats due to their venue location and customer service amenities. Routinely they are the highest priced tickets for sporting events. The capacity there is 45,971 including 4,631 club seats and 72 luxury suites, according to TheOrioles.com. The luxury suites accommodate 14–75 patrons each, according to the site, and for this revenue estimation this thesis will use the approximate average of 20 tickets purchased per suite per game. The suites range in price from $900-$5,000/game, which equates to a per person ticket cost ranging from $64-$67.

Such an idea for a tiered security fee could, for example, affix a $1 charge to all tickets, $2 for Club level seats and $3 for Suite patrons. Based on these numbers, a sold out Camden Yards would produce $39,900 in regular tickets, another $9,262 in Club level fees, and $4,320 from the Suites, totaling $53,482 per sold out game. If the team were to sell out all 81 home events, it would have 3.72 million patrons and accordingly this would produce $4.33 million annually in security fees. In 2013, however, Baltimore was slightly below the league average in attendance, generating 2,357,561 patrons or 29,105 per game. If pro-rating the projected security fee per game from the maximum possible above, this would yield 63% of seating capacity and a projected total of $2.74 million / year in security fees.

With 30 professional baseball clubs all generating similar revenues, it is logical to project the possibility of adding $82.2 million annually for security expenses including security systems upgrades, personnel training improvements, and security staff quantity increases. This example-generated revenue figure is solely based on adding a nominal security fee to MLB patrons, providing a voluntary tax supplemental fund. In 2013, MiLB generated another 41.2 million patrons; the NFL 17.3 million; NCAA football 50.3 million and NCAA basketball another 27.8 million across 657 university venues.[311]

Of course, for practical reasons and realistic implementation, a HSE Working Group could recommend a higher fee for congressional review and adoption by statute. As explained earlier, the aviation security fee originally imposed in 2002 had not been raised through 2013. However, Congress has now changed the fee structure in 2014 such that the fee is currently set at $5.60 per one way trip regardless of legs taken in the trip. This reflects some perspective on the amount of possible fees to consider for sporting event ticket purchases. Further, the original TSA security fee legislation required that the first $250 million acquired is mandatorily set aside for the Aviation Security Capital Fund which specifically provides for airport facility modifications and security

---

[311] Chris Huston, "NCAA Football Attendance Topped 50 Million for the First Time in 2013," *NBC Sports*, February 10, 2014, http://collegefootballtalk.nbcsports.com/2014/02/10/ncaa-football-attendance-topped-50-million-for-the-first-time-in-2013/; "2013 NCAA Football Records," NCAA, http://fs.ncaa.org/Docs/stats/football_records/2013/Attendance.pdf.

equipment.[312]   The Aviation Security Fee has served as an excellent example of a successful model directly tying revenues obtained to tangible security resources provided.

In addition to this, as with the TSA imposed airline security fees, there could be a similar fee levied on the private sector professional clubs and respective University Athletic Departments as well. These fees could be the subject of deliberative discussions and debate. But in the end, arriving at an agreeable fee structure with the private sector is not only possible, but likely given the fact that there would also be a public support incentive as well, to form a tri-lateral funding program based on the model in place for TSA and aviation industry security.

As addressed previously, FEMA has the HSGP funds that might include sports venue security. Between the SHSP and the UASI Grant programs, FEMA had $913.3 million for distribution in FY 13. If FEMA were to allocate only 2.19% of this budgeted Grant program, this would total $20 million annually toward SEAR 4–5 venue security improvements. Over the course of a possible five-year plan, this would generate $100 million toward the nation's public gathering venues in most dire need of support.

The concept of a shared responsibility is not new to professional sports. In the NFL, M&T Bank Stadium is the venue for the Baltimore Ravens. Building the stadium in 1996 cost $220 million; however, the funds were generated through a combination of proceeds from the sale of tax-exempt revenue bonds, new games established in the Maryland Lottery, and the Ravens football club. This is a routine method of resourcing for public-private ventures in the sports entertainment industry and is easily accepted as commonplace among industry patrons.

Yet another possible avenue for a collaborative effort is the model demonstrated in the U.K. with the FA Football Foundation. The Football Foundation is the UK's largest sports charity and is funded primarily by the Premier League (private-sector), The Football Association (NGO) and the Government. The foundation has routinely allocated £30m annually (approximately $45 million) into developing stadium renovations, soccer

---

[312] "The Transportation Security Administration and the Aviation Security Fee," U.S. House of Representatives, Committee on the Budget, Paul Ryan, Chairman, December 10, 2013, http://budget.house.gov/news/documentsingle.aspx?DocumentID=364049

facilities and youth programs.[313]   However, for 2014–2016, it will be allocating £50m (approximately $75 million) annually, according to the foundation's website, and focusing it on stadium renovations. The foundation also works to solicit private donors to leverage even more funding.

Whereas the foundation's mission is largely to renovate aging stadiums, enhance security capabilities, and build new athletic facilities for community involvement at the very lowest levels, it sets an example of the public-private partnership that might be possible between American organized sporting leagues, the NCAA, and the government to derive funding for SEAR 4–5 venues. Perhaps to entice public policy action, this kind of foundation could be set up to assist organizations build and develop community athletic facilities for underprivileged neighborhoods in cities. This could encourage participation from across cultures and demographics.

In this chapter, the thesis has analyzed voluminous research data and sources to provide and support responses to the three respective Research Questions. The findings have resolved that SEAR 4–5 sporting venues constitute viable, valuable soft targets susceptible to terrorist attacks. Additionally, in light of 21st century evolutions in communications and global media, dominance and exposure, these venues are likely to serve as a platform for proclaiming terrorist causes. This chapter also demonstrated a cost-benefit analysis that indicates sufficient rationale to consider select, cost-effective public policy options to fortify SEAR 4–5 event security. And finally, the chapter identified and briefly reviewed numerous public policy options ranging from little or no fiscal expense to those options that do include significant cost. In analyzing the more expensive options, this thesis has also provided numerous examples and models for innovative funding streams to minimize any government expense.

In the final chapter of this thesis, the problem statement will be re-visited and conclusions will be derived from the research, thereby serving to provide recommendations for further HSE research, review, and deliberation.

---

[313] David Conn, "FA Makes £150m Pledge to Improve Run-down Urban Facilities," *The Guardian*, February 25, 2013, http://www.theguardian.com/football/2013/feb/25/fa-premier-league-grassroots-facilities.

IV. SUMMARY

Mankind, it seems, makes a poorer performance of government than of almost any other human activity. In this sphere, wisdom, which may be defined as the exercise of judgment acting on experience, common sense and available information, is less operative and more frustrated than it should be. Why do holders of high office so often act contrary to the way reason points and enlightened self-interest suggests?

—Barbara Tuchman,
A March to Folly

A. RECOMMENDATIONS

The overarching conclusion of this thesis is the necessity for the federal government and private sector to build an exceptionally robust public-private collaboration to more successfully protect SEAR 4 and 5 sports venues from potential terrorist attacks. The following recommendations provide a viable range of options, which when implemented in full, will this partnership and strengthen existing security measures at these less nationally prominent yet vulnerable venues.

> Notwithstanding the security operations being executed by the private sector, there will be the need to integrate the setting of standards, to actively conduct compliance monitoring, to strategically plan and manage security operations, and to provide the overall synchronization of the twenty-first century's multi-agency, collaborative approach to homeland security.[314]

In 2011, this was a congressional statement regarding how aviation industry security should be reorganized from the federal sector into a private sector-based structure in order to decrease federal expenditures and increase efficiencies. Sporting venue security is already structured in such a private sector-reliant manner. In the following seven recommendations, this thesis advocates the same congressional ideal be

---

[314] U.S. House of Representatives Joint Majority Staff Report, "A Decade Later: A Call for TSA Reform" (Washington, DC: Congress, November 16, 2011), 20, http://oversight.house.gov/wp-content/uploads/2012/03/2011-11-16-TSA_Reform_Report.pdf.

applied to America's sports venues, but at a fraction of the cost of today's security in the transportation industry.

The recommendations of this thesis are listed in order of escalating cost and associated with increasing legislative and/or public resistance. The final recommendation, however, is in preparation for the future and involves no current fiscal expense. Provided here is a summary list of the recommendations with the lead agency/entity denoted; each recommendation is subsequently explained in greater detail:

1. Finalize and publish the National Protection Framework with a specified Annex for sporting event venue security (DHS)

2. Establish a streamlined office within HSE for inspection and compliance adherence (DHS)

3. Replicate U.K.'s organizational structure placing a federal Subject Matter Expert with state/local level personnel to synchronize security at the local level with the national level to improve operational harmonization (DHS)

4. Allocate 2.2% of the FEMA Grant budget annually for a five year plan dedicated to reduce security vulnerabilities at SEAR 4–5 venues nationwide (DHS)

5. Assess a statutory security fee on sporting event ticket purchases to fund enhanced SEAR 4–5 venue security, while acting to obtain patron stakeholder partnership with the government (DHS and Congress)

6. Create a charitable foundation to serve as a funding source dedicated to stadium infrastructure renovations to facilitate improved security for SEAR 4–5 events (Private sector)

7. Rapidly prepare for future use of CCTV facial recognition technology by addressing operational and legal concerns immediately (DHS)

Recommendation 1: Finalize and publish the National Protection Framework (NPF) with a specified Annex for sporting event venue security (DHS)

Current DHS policy does not intend to reach down into state/local LE operational realms, nor does it intend to direct how local policing can best be accomplished. However, it is essential for DHS to establish, finalize, and publish the NPF. But that is only a requisite beginning, as also needed is a public event protection mission doctrine, or Annex, that is specific enough to be useful at the local level and to provide consistency nationwide. The working draft NPF with general core capabilities listed is conducive to empowering the state/local LE communities to derive tailored doctrines. However, it is too broad and leaves room for disparate or limited regional local doctrines. In some areas of the NPF there is essentially no doctrine or uniform approach to sporting event venue protection issues. Further, the federal doctrine needs to provide an effective inspection or compliance mechanism. Local compliance must be an intrinsic component of any successful doctrine meant to responsibly ensure a national standard of protection is being met.

The sporting event Annex to the NPF should paint the ideal picture of what SEAR 4–5 event venue operational security should look like, i.e., the "how to" document to effect the partnership between DHS, private-sector, and state/local authorities (government and LE). Of course, this image would be provided to the extent possible understanding that each venue has characteristics and circumstances rendering it unique. However, as described in Chapter III, the Secret Service has established a widely used conceptual site strategy deploying outer, middle, and inner rings of security, albeit intended for the most high-profile major events.[315] Therefore, it would be extremely reasonable for the NPF Annex to echo and complement that conceptual strategy for application to SEAR 4–5 events.

The Annex should entail how the existing and future technologies (now in the prototype stage) will be used to complement each other in providing the over-lapping belts of security on-site. It should provide intent and guidance for deploying automobile X-ray equipment for parking facilities, ETD equipment placement on approaches to venue entry points, and CCTV surveillance and SOC procedures. And of practical importance, it can provide specificity as to new structural organization, intended working relationships, licensing process, and procedural means to attain funding and support from DHS. These specific matters are addressed in the additional following recommendations.

Recommendation 2: Establish a streamlined office within (DHS) for partnering, inspection, and compliance adherence (DHS)

Unfortunately, a frank economic truth is that private-sector profit routinely emanates from efficiency. Oftentimes, such streamlined operations entail lean staffing

---

[315] Connors, *Planning and Managing Security,* 33–37.

designs and reluctance to pay for cutting edge technologies. This equates to decisions made assuming more operational risk in order to spend less on security costs. In sum, it can be expected that the private sector will hope to strike a balance of how much to spend v. how much threat to protect against. However, a U.S. military adage is that "hope is not a course of action."

As demonstrated in Chapter III, the current reliance on the Best-Practice resources as a doctrinal strategy, dispersed haphazardly across the sports entertainment industry has resulted in inconsistent implementation, notable complacency, and overall systemic failure. The recommended office within DHS can be the oversight focal point to set terrorist response training standards, establish and monitor practice consistency nationwide, as well as to establish and issue licensure certifications.

With a suitable, measurable doctrine in place, it is necessary to provide a conduit for outreach/engagement, capacity development, and ensuring the inspection-compliance mechanism has the resources to be successfully executed.[316] There are various federal agencies that have field offices across the country and even in remote regions of the world with similar duties. One such existing office within DHS is TSA's Office of Global Strategies (TSA-OGS).[317] It is a proven, successful model for an office with oversight, compliance and partnership roles in the field. So it would not be unprecedented to establish this proposed DHS office for sports venue security and licensing oversight with personnel stationed in the field, embedded at the state/local level. The organizational mechanism for the licensing procedure is discussed in more detail in Recommendation 3 and the Implementation Plan, below.

Admittedly, there are other agencies, such as the FBI, JTTF, etc., that work with the state/local LE level to provide federal level operational support. However, these entities are not charged with the responsibility of measuring a national standard for executing the protection mission as is DHS. Therefore, the Department needs to have a

---

[316] These three facets of a proposed office align with the TSA Office of Global Strategies published mission areas. U.S. Transportation Security Administration (TSA), "Global Strategies," August 28, 2013, http://www.tsa.gov/stakeholders/global-strategies.

[317] TSA-OGS provides liaisons stationed in dozens of countries worldwide to meet the three goals cited above: outreach/engagement, capacity development, and inspection-compliance.

more active role regarding Protection Security doctrine and its compliance. A small centralized office is recommended to provide oversight as well as to partner with the public-private stakeholders at the local level to help them get to the desired standards. The personnel from this office will be stationed in the field, and their roles will be addressed in the following recommendation below.

Though likely an unpopular measure with the private sector, compliance with the standards should be linked to a national protection mission certification or license, like the one issued in the U.K. by the Football Licensing Authority, in order to prevent complacency from becoming the reason for terrorist success. As cited in Chapter III, elements within the law enforcement community already advocate legislation requiring licensing standards. Currently, the NCS4 at the University of Southern Mississippi offers a voluntary, Best Practice type "Sport Venue Staff Certification."[318] The certification targets venue staff and security team training and background-screening. The licensing procedure recommended in this thesis would begin with this program and add onto it select requirements for surveillance and detection equipment installation and training.

If the local level stakeholders encounter resource constraints in meeting standards, the newly dedicated DHS office would be the ideal conduit for multi-agency collaboration and multi-resource synchronization for solutions.

> **Recommendation 3:** Replicate select aspects of the U.K.'s organizational structure by embedding a federal Subject Matter Expert at the state/local level to synchronize with national level personnel to improve operational harmonization and better support local policing at sports venues (DHS)

Placing a federal Subject Matter Expert, such as the U.K.'s Football Liaison or Football Intelligence Officers at the state/local level specifically to synchronize and coordinate federal level support will improve operational harmonization. These personnel will be the face of DHS at the local level to act as the channel for multi-agency coordination and to confect professional trust and partnering with the private-sector for

---

[318] "Sports Venue Staff Certification," National Center for Spectator Sports Safety and Security, accessed April 2, 2014, http://www.ncs4.com/csvs.

procedural compliance. Currently, there is no such equivalent at the Fusion Centers or state/local level.

Currently, the JTTF does have operational personnel at the state/local level. However, the DHS structure down to the local level would not be operationally oriented in the same manner as the JTTF SMEs. Instead, the DHS presence is recommended to be more of a specified FLO or FIO type of position that the U.K. has immersed successfully at the local police department level. Such a resource can focus specifically on the sports and entertainment industry schedule through the course of a year and continually coordinate with Fusion Centers, JTTF, state/local LE, and venue security teams.

Though this is an option involving staffing expenditures, Chapters II and III have revealed the extent of the successful practice in the U.K. Having people on the ground at the local level building trust, establishing rapport, and directly linking that to national level resources and leadership will go a long way to cover the gap of inconsistent standards now present in the field. Strategically embedding the DHS presence at the local level will be critical to synchronizing this recommended system because it is local policing, local police departments, and local venues that serve on the front lines of the national protection mission.

As explained in the comparison section of Chapter II, though there are many more police departments in the U.S. than in the U.K., the roles for these DHS FLO/FIO type positions embedded at the local level would not be positioned at every police department responsible for a venue as is the case in the U.K. Rather, these personnel would serve the dual purpose to operate a "train the trainer" program. These DHS personnel in the field would routinely go on-location to venues throughout each state to provide much needed training and exercise support to venue security teams. Partnering with local LE and first responder agencies will empower the venue security teams to consistently maintain their protection mission-based counterterrorism and operational readiness.

As revealed in previous chapters, there is no current protection mission doctrine. The DHS office recommended above should provide that doctrinal guidance and develop this "train the trainer" strategy for the embedded SMEs to coordinate. The SMEs should then collaborate with and deliver course materials to local LE and private-sector security teams so that they can be self-sufficient to maintain their doctrinal compliance and operational proficiency to standard. Recommendations 4–6, below, specifically address funding innovations to alleviate the fiscal expense for this proposed organizational structure.

These DHS personnel embedded at the local level would also serve the invaluable function to facilitate the outreach/engagement to and from the local level with the federal level to work through regional specific issues. They would serve as the conduit previously mentioned to expand mission capacity development, procuring funds for equipment and training support. Finally, these DHS SMEs would dispel the daunting notion of externally based "federal inspectors" periodically appearing from "inside the beltway" to assure compliance. The embedded DHS personnel would partner, side-by-side, with the state/local authorities and private-sector entities to routinely, closely collaborate to mitigate vulnerabilities, meet and maintain the requisite standards for the issuance of a security license authorizing venues for sporting events.

A key element of this recommendation is to create a credible, seamless partnership with the state/local LE and private sector at the local level to facilitate meeting standards and enhancing security at the SEAR 4–5 events

> **Recommendation 4:** Allocate 2.2% of the FEMA Grant budget annually for a five-year plan dedicated to reducing security vulnerabilities at SEAR 4–5 venues nationwide (DHS)

As illustrated in Chapter III, the Transit Security Grant Program (TSGP) serves as a model for administering a sector-specific funding stream in support of counterterrorism security. Based on the example cost-benefit analysis conducted in Chapter III, DHS should allocate 2.2% ($20 million annually) of the total FEMA HSGP budget for a five year plan to earmark $100 million for SEAR 4–5 venue security. These earmarked funds would not be adding to overall federal expense because the HSGP funding is already in the federal budget.

Also demonstrated in Chapter III, successful precedent has been established for statutorily dedicating funding to facility renovation and surveillance/detection equipment procurement. The current TSA Security Fee statutorily channels $250 million annually specifically toward airport facility renovation and equipment purchase and upgrades.[319] Like the statutory requirements in place for TSA now, this recommended FEMA five year plan would help empower SEAR 4–5 security teams with the purchase of CCTV equipment, EDT technology systems, establishing SOCs, and establishing training and operational exercises at venues nationwide.

Further, the value of the ETD (PHASE) technology breakthrough recounted in Chapter II cannot be underestimated. As explained on p. 25, ETD equipment with a proven effective 100M stand-off range will be an invaluable addition to the HSE fight against IED attacks. This technology should be funded and fielded as absolutely soon as possible. Therefore, funding should be invested immediately to expedite its path toward production. Though the cost of the marketable PHASE ETD system is not yet established, it soon will be, and the benefit that the HSE and the public could reap from its success may prove priceless. Such a landmark breakthrough will certainly prove to be a key weapon on which SEAR 4–5 venue security teams will rely to accomplish the 21st century HSE protection mission.

> **Recommendation 5:** Assess a statutory security fee on sporting event ticket purchases to fund enhanced SEAR 4–5 venue security, while acting to obtain patron stakeholder partnership with the government (DHS and Congress)

This recommendation focuses on obtaining spectator-patron buy-in to partner with the government and private sector for funding SEAR 4–5 venue security. As shown in Chapter III, the sports entertainment industry has massive customer base and economic scope. This, coupled with the rare industry attribute of possessing a potentially enormous funding base from its own patrons (like the aviation travel industry), enables it to partner in the funding of expanding security resources and operations for its own advantage.

The innovative idea to assess a Security Fee to sporting event ticket purchases will essentially constitute a voluntary tax that will be paid by the concurrence of the people benefitting the most from its existence. Not only could such a Security Fee be

---

[319] TSA, "Transit Security Grant Program." The FY 2014 Transit Security Grant Program was initially authorized in Section 1406 of the Implementing Recommendations of the 9/11 Commission Act of 2007, Public Law 110–53 (6 U.S.C. 1135) and is currently funded under Public Law No: 113–76, H.R.3547 – Consolidated Appropriations Act, 2014.

applied to ticket purchases but also to parking lot pricing in order to help allocate funds toward automobile X-ray equipment for use at the venue parking facilities. The data used in the earlier examples demonstrate that the additional burden of cost on the consumer base is unlikely to adversely impact the private sector's sales or profit level.

As seen in Chapter III, future equipment implementation and personnel training expenditures can largely be offset through assessing a nominal security fee per each ticket sold. Surveys can be conducted and further research completed to determine specific consumer acceptability levels and price-break data in order to arrive at the optimally effective but least intrusive fee to be assessed. With the requisite goal to minimize consumer impact, even the simplified tier-model approach demonstrated and explained in Chapter III could be employed.

Positive spectator opinion and support is realistically achievable for several reasons. First, America's travelling public has come to accept the normalcy of the litany of fees assessed on airline tickets now. Further, the sports ticket buying public has also accepted the purely for profit convenience fees already attached to sporting event ticket prices. Providing visible, directly tangible improved sporting venue security measures that are initiated and maintained for spectator benefit will provide them with something to show for the nominal fee.

> **Recommendation 6:** Create a charitable foundation to serve as a funding source dedicated to stadium infrastructure renovations to facilitate improved security for SEAR 4–5 events (Private sector)

As explained in answering Research Question 3, the U.K.'s Football Foundation sets an excellent example from which the U.S. sports entertainment industry can glean valuable insight. If the spectator population may be required to contribute toward offsetting the costs of improved security training and equipment at SEAR 4–5 event venues, then the private-sector can also be an equal partner in the tripartite funding plan.

The private-sector sporting club ownership groups and even the collegiate athletic departments nationwide can lead by example partnering to set-up and manage a charitable foundation benefitting the long-term future of the industry, its participants and its spectators. Plus with it bearing a charitable status, there will be ample incentive and marketing strategies that can be employed to increase its value to the public and benefit to the HSE.

The U.K. model functions to raise money to overhaul aging stadiums and to provide new facilities for learning and playing the game in underprivileged metropolitan neighborhoods and in remote regions of the nation. In the English Premier (Soccer) League, the club ownership groups and the Football Association, as the NGO, have partnered to contribute £150 million (approximately $225 million) over the next 3 years.[320] Establishing such a high-profile fundraising role for the benefit of the sporting industry's patrons, as is now the case in the U.K., is a "good news story." Adapting this to the American sporting industry, demonstrating private-sector partnership in bearing fiscal burden, will further support the likelihood of spectator "buy-in" to a statutorily enacted security fee attached to ticket purchases.

Recommendation 7: Promptly prepare for future use of CCTV facial recognition technology by addressing operational and legal concerns immediately (DHS)

The last recommendation of this thesis, preparing for the use of CCTV facial recognition technology, allows time for the technology to evolve to a requisite state of negating or vastly minimizing the prospect of false-positive alarms. The false-positive alarms, as illustrated in the Analysis chapter, yield myriad operational and legal issues that the HSE is not yet prepared to address and overcome.

However, it is important to note that within the private sector, products such as FaceTrac are quickly making advances to technology which will minimize false positive alarm rates. In concluding with the last of the recommendations, it is necessary to acknowledge the legal and operational questions regarding facial recognition CCTV raised in Chapter III. Each of these will need to have organized responses prepared for now and ready to publish when the technology "catches up," or becomes suitable for the HSE protection mission to employ.

The plethora of questions previously raised includes: Where is the line to be drawn as to what citizen photo identification comparison database will be used? Will it include only individuals on the No Fly List? Will it include KSTs or an FBI, other federal level, or state/local LE criminal database? What specific access will private

---

[320] Conn, "FA Makes £150m Pledge."

sector security employees have to that database? Even if no private sector employee access to that database is granted, then what is the sequence of events when the alarm sounds in the SOC recognizing a "match" with one of the comparison databases? What of the actions to be taken? Has any operational coordination been completed between federal and state/local LE levels to preclude confronting a KST only to destroy what may be months or years of work by another agency in monitoring or tracking that individual?

The bottom line is that the HSE needs to prepare now for when facial recognition CCTV technology products are ready to be a valuable resource to the national protection mission and can then be utilized at SEAR 4 and 5 sporting events. Therefore, it is essential for the HSE to move quickly in its preparations for the coming day when the technological breakthrough will call for immediate implementation at SEAR 4 and 5 sports venues.

B.   IMPLEMENTATION PLAN

In order to render these recommendations a reality, several steps are necessary in the near term and long term future.

The first step is for DHS to form a Working Group across Department and Agency borders. It is essential to remove the idea of such creative solutions from the abyss of the federal stove-pipe syndrome, where ideas are thought of and conceived simultaneously but without coordination, i.e., repeating the same efforts and wasting time and resources in so doing.

This Working Group (WG) should examine the nuances of the issues raised and further research the shaping of the thesis recommendations. The WG will also bear the responsibility and authority to form a collective judgment not only regarding doctrinal revisions and additions, but for deriving new HSE organizational structures and working relationships, assessing technological capabilities, and laying the groundwork for the innovative funding streams recommended. These actions would tremendously serve the people by evaluating and planning for the future development of where, when, and how to stop terrorist attacks in America.

The WG must be expansive enough to be insightful but not bloated to the point of inaction or inability to move at anything more than glacial speed. Preparations are needed now for technology innovations on the cusp of becoming reality in the market. More importantly, as facility managers already perceive, it is just a matter of time before attacks occur at SEAR 4–5 venues. The WG must move forward with purpose. Therefore, representation on the WG will be needed from:

- Professional sports league Security Directors from MLB, NFL, NBA, NHL, and MLS;

- Three select NCAA Security Directors, such as one each from the Southeastern Conference, the Big 10, and the Pac 12;

- The state/local law enforcement community, such as the Association of Chiefs of Police, several major metropolitan Police Chiefs such as from New York, Boston, and Dallas, as well as a few select State Police Chiefs;

- Federal law enforcement SMEs from the FBI and JTTF;

- Intelligence Community representation, i.e., one or two SMEs from any of ODNI, NSA, CIA, DHS-OI and/or NPPD;

- The Academic community, with a representative from the two leading centers for sports venue security study at the University of South Carolina and Southern Mississippi University

A WG of these 18–20 representatives with DHS HQ synchronization will serve as an excellent resource base of Subject Matter Expertise and be reflective of an industry-wide partnership with the HSE.

Though the thesis recommendations may incur some modicum of cost for the most ambitious applications, the WG can fully analyze the investment for long-term security. As demonstrated in Chapter III, staying ahead of the imminent next steps of the terrorists will be far more worthy an investment than scrambling to form a knee-jerk security response after many have perished at one or more of America's soft-target SEAR 4–5 sporting venues.

Because even state and local agencies in the U.S. are facing austere fiscal climates, the burden of the training for local law enforcement and private sector security teams can be shared with the federal government. The WG can advocate congressional action to grant private sector incentives, statutory fees, and FEMA funding for training venue security team employees how to use world class technology and to conduct training to standard in the roles as emergency first responders, as is done in the U.K. Such funding for training can be used by DHS for conferences and forums that continue to push constantly developing technology and collaboration in the security industry. With such equipment and SOC precision planning possible, the security workforce executing the operations plans must receive comparable quality training.

The WG will also serve as the initial collaborative planning body for the operational partnership between federal and state/local levels. It will establish the roles and responsibilities for the federal embedded personnel and make determinations as to where these people will work daily, such as at Fusion Centers or in Police Departments. The WG can also complete detailed reviews of other functional and logistically practical aspects of implementation.

So it is imperative that DHS establish the Working Group to explore the possibilities recommended in this thesis, to ensure the HSE is making its fullest effort to accomplish its Homeland Security protection mission.

C. CONCLUSION

> *We will always remember. We will always be proud. We will always be prepared, so we will always be free.*

—Ronald Reagan,
40th U.S. president

Just because a well-orchestrated, multiple coordinated IED attack has not yet reigned catastrophe at America's smaller sports venues, does not mean that the United States Government should not take prudent, sage steps forward to prepare a defense for that imminent terrorist strategy. The NCTC considers this a worst case scenario, and so too should DHS.

The thesis problem statement indicated that there will continue to be terrorists in the American homeland and there are currently potential sports venue targets that are vastly softer than others. The research questions diagnosed that SEAR 4–5 rated sporting

117

events are such a viable, valuable, and vulnerable soft target; that there are quantitative cost-benefit means available to analyze possible solutions; and that there are numerous public policy options available at no cost, little cost, or innovatively funded minimal costs to consider for implementation. This thesis has recommended action now, both for mending the gaps in security in the present, as well as for preparing for well-reasoned, long-term solutions for the future.

If the Department of Homeland Security is to win not only in the close-in, current battle against terrorism, but also in the deep, future battle against terrorism as well, then it must take time to recognize the status-quo of its protection mission posture as insufficient to meet the threat of an ever-increasingly more sophisticated enemy. Such status-quo recognition will illuminate where increased protection is needed today and paths forward tomorrow. DHS should proactively pursue and act on the recommendations provided in this thesis by establishing a professional Working Group to improve on the HSE protection mission of sports venues today and move aggressively into the future, before the enemy does.

LIST OF REFERENCES

American Science & Engineering (AS&E). "American Science and Engineering, Inc. Receives $4.5 Million Order for Z Portal and Gemini X-ray Systems to Secure Checkpoints at Middle Eastern University." October 1, 2013. http://ir.as-e.com/releasedetail.cfm?releaseid=794210.

Anderson, Teresa. "How Dallas Does Security." *Security Management*, 2010. http://www.securitymanagement.com/article/how-dallas-does-security-007656.

Andreeva, Nellie. "Full 2010–11 Season Series Rankings," *Deadline: Hollywood,* May 2, 2011.

Arnaut, José Luis. *Independent European Sport Review 2006.* UK Presidency of the EU 2005, October 2006.

Associated Press. "MLB Attendance Drops 1.2 Percent This Year." *USA Today*, October 1, 2013. http://www.usatoday.com/story/sports/mlb/2013/10/01/mlb-attendance-drops-12-percent-this-year/2904661/.

———. "Number of Smartphones Expected to Triple to 5.6 Billion by 2019." *The Washington Times*, November 11, 2013. http://www.washingtontimes.com/news/2013/nov/11/number-smartphones-expected-triple-56-billion-2019/.

Association of Chief Police Officers (ACPO). *Guidance on Policing Football.* London: National Policing Improvement Agency, 2010. http://www.acpo.police.uk/documents/uniformed/2010/201008UNGPF01.pdf.

Bardach, Eugene. *A Practical Guide for Policy Analysis: The Eightfold Path to More Effective Problem Solving.* 4th ed. Washington, DC: CQ Press, 2011.

Bauder, David. "Online Offerings Transform Olympic Experience." *Associated Press*. February 12, 2014. http://wintergames.ap.org/article/online-offerings-transform-olympic-experience.

BBC News. "Football Violence on the Rise." August 15, 2001. http://news.bbc.co.uk/2/hi/uk_news/1491743.stm.

Bickel, Robert D. *Legal Issues Related To Silent Video Surveillance.* Washington, D.C.: The Security Industry Association and The Private Sector Liaison Committee, April 8, 1999.

Blanton, Dana. "Fox News Poll: Most Voters Glad They Know Snowden Secrets." *Fox News*, January 22, 2014. http://www.foxnews.com/politics/2014/01/22/fox-news-poll-most-voters-glad-know-snowden-secrets/.

Blodgett, Henry. "The Number of Smartphones in Use is about to Pass the Number of PCs." *Business Insider*, December 11, 2013. http://www.businessinsider.com/ number-of-smartphones-tablets-pcs-2013-12.

Brannan, David W., and N. T. Anders Strindberg. *Critical Analysis of Terrorism and Terrorist Groups: A Handbook for Practitioners*. Unpublished paper. 2013.

Brioux, Bill. "Olympic TV Ratings Down from Vancouver, but Online Numbers Soar: Daily TV Average Dropped from Four Million Viewers to 1.5 Million." *The Canadian Press*, February 25, 2014. http://www.canada.com/entertainment/ Olympic+ratings+down+from+Vancouver+online+numbers+soar/9549618/story. html.

Brooks, Tim, and Earle Marsh. *The Complete Directory to Prime Time Network and Cable TV Shows, 1946-Present*. (New York: Ballantine, 2007).

Candiotti, Susan. "Suspect: Boston Bombing was Payback for Hits on Muslims." *CNN*, May 17, 2013. http://www.cnn.com/2013/05/16/us/boston-bombing-investigation/.

Canetti, Elias. *Masse und Macht*. Hamburg: Claassen, 1960.

Carey, Bill. "Stadium Security Continues to Evolve 10 Years After 9/11." *SI.com*, September 9, 2001. http://sportsillustrated.cnn.com/2011/more/09/06/stadium .security.changes.since.9.11/.

Caudle, Sharon. "Homeland Security: Advancing the National Strategic Position." *Homeland Security Affairs* 8 (August 2012). http://www.hsaj.org/ ?article=8.1.11.

Chapman, Clark R., and Alan W. Harris. "A Skeptical Look at September 11th." *Skeptical Inquirer* 26, no. 5 (2002).

Conn, David. "FA Makes £150m Pledge to Improve Run-down Urban Facilities." *The Guardian*, February 25, 2013. http://www.theguardian.com/football/2013/feb/25/ fa-premier-league-grassroots-facilities.

Connors, Edward. *Planning and Managing Security for Major Special Events: Guidelines for Law Enforcement*. Alexandria, VA: Institute for Law and Justice, March 2007.

Crenshaw, Martha. "Innovation: Decision Points in the Trajectory of Terrorism." Paper presented at the Conference on Trajectories of Terrorist Violence in Europe, Harvard University, Cambridge, Massachusetts, March 9–11, 2001.

Defense Daily. "Defense Daily, An Access Intelligence, LLC Service." May 23, 2012. http://www.defensedaily.com/Assets/File/txt/TR2_2012-05-22_14-31.txt.

Economist, The. "If Looks Could Kill." October 23, 2008. http://www.economist.com/node/12465303.

Edwards, Jim. "TV Is Dying, and Here Are The Stats That Prove It." *Business Insider*, November 24, 2013.

Ericson, Richard V., and Aaron Doyle. *Uncertain Business: Risk, Insurance and the Limits of Knowledge*. Toronto: University of Toronto Press, 2004.

Federal Emergency Management Agency (FEMA). *Working Draft—National Protection Framework, Review Package, Presidential Policy Directive/PPD-8*. Washington, DC: FEMA, March 2012.

Fisher, Kathryn. "From 20th Century Troubles to 21st Century International Terrorism: Identity, Securitization, and British Counterterrorism from 1968 to 2011." Ph.D dissertation, The London School of Economics and Political Science, 2012.

Fleece, Richard. "Suicide Terrorism in America?: The Complex Social Conditions of this Phenomenon and the Implications for Homeland Security." Master's thesis, Naval Postgraduate School, December 2012.

Giannopoulos, Georgios, Roberto Filippini, and Muriel Schimmer. *Risk Assessment Methodologies for Critical Infrastructure Protection: Part I, A State of the Art*. Luxembourg: Publications Office of the European Union, 2012.

Goss, Benjamin D., Jubenville, Colby B., and Jon L. MacBeth. *Primary Principles of Post-9/11 Stadium Security in the United States: Transatlantic Implications from British Practices*. International Association of Assembly Managers, June 2003.

Granholm, Jennifer M. "Video Surveillance on Public Streets: The Constitutionality of Invisible Citizen Searches." *University of Detroit Law Review* 4, no. 64 (1987): 687–713.

Griggs, Gerald. "Soccer Hooliganism in England between the Wars." *The Sport Journal* 7, no. 3 (2004): 1–5. http://www.thesportjournal.org/article/soccer-hooliganism-england-between-wars.

Hafez, Mohammed M., and Maria Rasmussen. *Terrorist Innovations in Weapons of Mass Effect, Phase II*. PASCC Report Number 2012 003. Monterey, CA: Naval Postgraduate School, Center on Contemporary Conflict, January 2012.

Haley, A. J. "British Soccer Superhooligans: Emergence and Establishment: 1982–2000." *The Sport Journal* 4, no. 3 (2001). http://web.archive.org/web/20070221100029/http://www.thesportjournal.org/2001Journal/Vol4-No3/soccer-hooligans.asp.

Hall, Stacey A. "An Examination of British Sport Security Strategies, Legislation, and Risk Management Practices: Lessons Learned from the English Football League." *The Sport Journal* 13, no. 2 (2010): 1–7. http://www.thesportjournal.org/article/examination-british-sport-security-strategies-legislation-and-risk-management-practices.

Hall, Stacey A., Lou Marciani, Walter Cooper, and Robert Rolen. "Securing Collegiate Sport Stadiums in the 21st Century: Think Security, Enhance Safety." *Homeland Security Institute, Journal of Homeland Security* (August 2007). https://www.hsdl.org/?view&did=30643.

Haupt, Robert. "Photoacoustic Sensing of Explosives." *Tech Notes*. November 2013. http://www.ll.mit.edu/publications/technotes/TechNote_PHASE.pdf.

Hoffman, Bruce. "Defending America against Suicide Terrorism." in *Three Years After: Next Steps in the War on Terror*, edited by David Aaron, 21–24. Santa Monica, CA: RAND, 2005.

———. *Inside Terrorism*. New York: Columbia University Press, 2006.

Hurst, Ronald E., Catherine Pratsinakis, and Paul H. Zoubek. "American Sports As A Target of Terrorism: The Duty of Care after September 11th." *Martindale.com*, May 1, 2003. http://www.martindale.com/legal-library/Article_Abstract.aspx?an=entertainment-sports&id=2342.

Huston, Chris. "NCAA football attendance topped 50 million for the first time in 2013," *NBC Sports*, February 10, 2014, http://collegefootballtalk.nbcsports.com/2014/02/10/ncaa-football-attendance-topped-50-million-for-the-first-time-in-2013.

International Association of Chiefs of Police (IACP), Community Oriented Policing Services (COPS). *Building Private Security/Public Policing Partnerships to Prevent and Respond to Terrorism and Disorder*. Washington, DC: U.S. Department of Justice, 2004. http://www.cops.usdoj.gov/mime/open.pdf?Item=1355.

Jenkins, Brian M. *Will Terrorists Go Nuclear?* P-5541. Santa Monica, CA: RAND, November 1975.

Johns, Greg. "Safeco Field Adding Metal Detectors for Added Security." *MLB.com*, January 21, 2014. http://mlb.mlb.com/news/article/mlb/fans-to-pass-through-metal-detectors-at-safeco-field-beginning-this-season?ymd=20140121&content_id=66900582&vkey=news_mlb.

Johnson, Gary. "NCAA Attendance Hits New High." *NCAA.com*, January 26, 2012. http://www.ncaa.com/news/football/article/2012-01-26/ncaa-attendance-hits-new-high.

Journés, Claude. "Policing and Security: Terrorists and Hooligans." *Sport In Society* 1, no. 2 (1998): 145–60.

Keating, Peter. "Industry of Fear." *ESPN The Magazine*, September 11, 2011. http://espn.go.com/espn/story/_/id/6936819/stadiums-increase-budgets-heighten-security-measures-protect-fans-espn-magazine.

Kenber, Billy. "Nidal Hasan Convicted of Ft. Hood Killings." *Washington Post*, August, 23, 2013.

King, Rob. "Olympics Run £2 Billion Over-Budget as Security Costs Double Due to Poor Planning." *Daily Mail*. March 9, 2012, http://www.dailymail.co.uk /news/article-2112489/London-2012-Olympics-runs-2bn-budget-security-costs-double.html.

Kinnvall, Catarina. "Globalization and Religious Nationalism: Self, Identity, and the Search for Ontological Security." *Political Psychology* 25, no. 5 (2004): 741–767.

Lewis, Jeffrey W. *The Business of Martyrdom: A History of Suicide Bombing*. Annapolis, MD: Naval Institute Press, 2012.

Lhotsky, Gary Joseph. "An Analysis of Risk Management at NCAA Division I-A Football Stadiums." Paper 3082. PhD diss., Florida State University, 2005. http://diginole.lib.fsu.edu/cgi/viewcontent.cgi?article=3016&context=etd.

Malik, Om., "Happy Birthday MLB.TV. Now That's What I Call Sports TV," GIGAOM. August 26, 2012. http://gigaom.com/2012/08/26/happy-10th-birthday-mlb-tv-now-thats-what-i-call-sports-tv/.

Marsh, James, Anne Fox, Kate Fox, Giovanni Carnibella, Joe McCann, and Peter Marsh. *Football Violence in Europe*. The Amsterdam Group, July 1996.

McCahill, Michael, and Clive Norris. *CCTV Systems in London. Their Structure and Practices*. Working Paper No.10. Hull, UK: Centre for Criminology and Criminal Justice, University of Hull, April 2003. http://www.urbaneye.net/results/ ue_wp10.pdf.

McLellan, Malcolm, III. "Tailoring Screening Technology to Prevent or Deter Terrorists from Attacking Commercial Ferries with Improvised Explosive Devices." Master's thesis, Naval Postgraduate School, 2010.

McMahon, Bill. Interview with Edward Norris and Steve Davis. *Norris and Davis Show*. CBS, WJZ-FM, January 27, 2014.

McNeil, Alex. *Total Television*. 4th ed. New York: Penguin, 1996.

Miller, John and Adam Dunn. "Perceptions of Terrorist Threat: Implications for Intercollegiate Basketball Venue Managers." *Journal of Venue and Entertainment Management* 3, no. 1 (July 2011): 1–10.

MIT Lincoln Laboratory. "MIT Lincoln Laboratory Wins Two R&D 100 Awards," July 2013, http://www.ll.mit.edu/news/2013-RnD100awards.html.

Moghaddam, Fathali M. *From the Terrorists' Point of View: What They Experience and Why They Come to Destroy.* Westport, CT: Greenwood, 2006.

Morag, Nadav. *Homeland Security in Israel: Counterterrorism Strategies.* Monterey, CA: Naval Postgraduate School, Center for Homeland Defense and Security, 2011.

Mosier, Jeff. "The Cost of Cowboys Stadium Has Escalated to $1.2 Billion." *The Dallas Morning News*, April 1, 2010. http://stadiumblog.dallasnews.com/2010/04/the-cost-of-cowboys-stadium-ha.html.

Mueller, John. "Six Rather Unusual Propositions about Terrorism." *Terrorism and Political Violence* 4, no. 17 (2005): 487–505. doi: 10.1080/095465591009359.

Mueller, John, and Mark G. Stewart. *Terror, Security, and Money: Balancing the Risks, Benefits, and Costs of Homeland Security.* New York: Oxford University Press, 2011.

Murray, Peter. "IATA Unveils The Airport Checkpoint Of The Future." *Singularity Hub.* June 28, 2011. http://singularityhub.com/2011/06/28/iata-unveils-the-airport-checkpoint-of-the-future/.

National Center for Spectator Sports Safety and Security (NCS4). "Intercollegiate Athletics Summit." January 2014. https://www.ncs4.com/summit/overview.

National Consortium for the Study of Terrorism and Responses to Terrorism (START). *Fact Sheet: Violent Extremism in the U.S.* College Park, MD: START, December 9, 2011.

———. *Background Report: Terrorism and the Olympics.* College Park, MD: START, July 2012.

Ngak, Chenda. "Boston Marathon Investigation: Are CCTV Cameras the Answer?" *CBS News*, April 16, 2013. http://www.cbsnews.com/news/boston-marathon-investigation-are-cctv-cameras-the-answer/.

Nieto, Marcus, Kimberly Johnston-Dodds and Charlene Wear Simmons, "Public and Private Applications of Video Surveillance," California Research Bureau, February 6, 2006, www.library.ca.gov/crb/02/06/02-006.pdf.

124

Oh, Onook, Agrawal Manish, and H. Raghav Rao. "Information Control and Terrorism: Tracking the Mumbai Terrorist Attack through Twitter." *Information Systems Frontiers* 14, no. 1 (March 2011): 33–43. doi: 10.1007/s10796-010-9275-8.

Pantera, M. J. III, R. Accorsi, C. Winter, R. Gobeille, S Griveas, D. Queen, J. Insalaco, and B. Domanoski. "Best Practices for Game Day Security at Athletic & Sport Venues." *The Sport Journal* 6, no. 4 (2003). http://www.thesportjournal.org/ article/best-practices- game-day-security-athletic-sport.

Pawlowski, A. "Is This the Checkpoint of the Future?" *CNN.com*, June 7, 2011. http://articles.cnn.com/2011-06-07/travel/checkpoint.of.the.future_1_airport-checkpoint-airport-security-traveler-program?_s=PM:TRAVEL.

Pape, Robert A., and James K. Feldman. *Cutting the Fuse: The Explosion of Global Suicide Terrorism and How to Stop It*. Chicago: University of Chicago Press, 2010.

Port Technology International. "U.S. CBP Places $19.3 Million Follow-on Order for AS&E's Z Backscatter Vans ZBVs." October 21, 2009. http://www.porttechnology.org/news/us_cbp_places_193_million_follow_on_ord er_for_ases_z_backscatter_vans_zbvs.

R&D Magazine, "Detecting Explosives Remotely" August 29, 2013, http://www.rdmag.com/award-winners/2013/08/detecting-explosives-remotely.

Reidl, Brian M. *50 Examples of Government Waste*. Washington, DC. The Heritage Foundation, October 6, 2009. http://www.heritage.org/research/reports/2009/10 /50-examples-of-government-waste#_edn45.

Reuters. "London 2012 —Final cost of London 2012 Games revealed." *Yahoo! Sport UK & Ireland*. October 23, 2012. http://uk.eurosport.yahoo.com/news/london-2012-final-cost-london-2012-games-revealed-135956051.html.

Schütz, Philip, Friedewald, Michael, Hallinan, Dara, Goos, Kerstin, and Jana Schuhmacher. *Smart Surveillance and Securing Public Spaces*. SAPIENT Report # 261698. Germany: Fraunhofer ISI, 2012. https://www.hsdl.org/ ?view&did=734129.

SecurLinx Corporation. "FaceTrac Surveillance System Pricing." Accessed February 1, 2014. http://www.securlinx.com/BR/pdf_files/FaceTrac%20Data%20Sheet.pdf.

Security Sales & Integration. "Research Firm Expects Bombings in Boston to Spur CCTV Spending." April 29, 2013. http://www.securitysales.com/article/research-firm-expects-bombings-in-boston-to-spur-cctv-spending/ Boston_Marathon_Bombings.

Seidman, Robert. "List of How Many Homes Each Cable Network Is In – As of August 2013." *TV by the Numbers*. August 23, 2013.

Shillinglaw, James. "IATA to Focus on Fast Travel, Checkpoint of the Future to Improve Air Travel." *TravelPulse*. October 16, 2012. http://www.travelpulse.com/iata-to-focus-on-fast-travel-checkpoint-of-the-future-to-improve-air-travel.html.

SiriusXM. "XM Satellite Radio Holdings Inc. - Current Report." January 9, 2004. http://investor.siriusxm.com/secfiling.cfm?filingID=1104659-04-473&CIK=1091530.

———. "SiriusXM Reports 2012 Results." February 5, 2013. http://investor.siriusxm.com/releasedetail.cfm?ReleaseID=737857.

———. "Sirius XM Exceeds 2013 Net Subscriber Target; Issues 2014 Subscriber And Free Cash Flow Guidance." January 7, 2014. http://investor.siriusxm.com/releasedetail.cfm?ReleaseID=817666.

Spinella, Edmund. *Biometric Scanning Technologies: Finger, Facial and Retinal Scanning*. Bethesda, MD: SANS Institute, May 28, 2003. http://www.sans.org/reading-room/whitepapers/authentication/biometric-scanning-technologies-finger-facial-retinal-scanning-1177.

Sports Business Daily. "Tailgating: Behind the Numbers." November 2012. http://www.sportsbusinessdaily.com/SB-Blogs/Events/Motorsports-Marketing-Forum/2012/11/Nascar-Tailgate-Graphic.aspx.

———. "Grapefruit, Cactus Leagues See Average Spring Training Attendance Drop." April 5, 2013. http://www.sportsbusinessdaily.com/Daily/Issues/2013/04/05/Research-and-Ratings/Spring-Training.aspx.

Tarlow, Peter E. *Event Risk Management and Safety*. New York: Wiley, 2002.

Toohey, Kristine. "Terrorism, Sport and Public Policy in the Risk Society." *Sport in Society* 11, no. 4 (2008): 429–42. doi: 10.1080/17430430802019367.

Nielsen Company, The. "Television at a Glance: Featuring a Look at Recent Consumer Traffic in Social Settings." Summer 2008, *TVbytheNumbers.zap2it.com*. http://tvbythenumbers.zap2it.com/wp-content/uploads/2008/08/summer2008.jpg.

Thiesen, Lisa, David Hannum, Dale Murray, and John Parmeter. "Survey of Commercially Available Explosives Detection Technologies and Equipment." Albuquerque, NM: Sandia National Laboratories, 2004.

United Kingdom, Department of Culture, Media and Sport. *London 2012 Olympic and Paralympic Games Quarterly Report—October 2012*. London: UK Department of Culture, Media and Sport, October 2012.

United Kingdom, Home Office. *The United Kingdom's Strategy for Countering International Terrorism.* Command Paper Number Cm 7547. London: United Kingdom Home Office, March 24, 2009. https://www.hsdl.org /?view&did=32602.

U.S. Congress. House, Joint Majority Staff Report. "A Decade Later: A Call for TSA Reform." Washington, DC: U.S. Congress, November 16, 2011. http://oversight.house.gov/wp-content/uploads/2012/03/2011-11-16-TSA_Reform_Report.pdf.

U.S. Customs and Border Protection (CBP). "Fact Sheet: Z-Portal Vehicle Imaging System." August 2008. http://www.cbp.gov/linkhandler/cgov/newsroom/ fact_sheets/port_security/z_portal.ctt/z_portal.pdf.

U.S. Department of Homeland Security (DHS). *Interim National Preparedness Goal, Homeland Security Presidential Directive 8: National Preparedness.* Washington, DC: DHS, March 31, 2005.

———. "Bomb Threat Stand-off Chart." March 20, 2009. https://www.llis.dhs.gov/sites/default/files/DHS-BombThreatChart-6-5-09.pdf.

———. *Defining Video Quality Requirements: A Guide for Public Safety,* Washington, DC: DHS, May 2013.

———. *Overview of the National Planning Frameworks.* Washington, DC: DHS, May 1, 2013.

———. *Quadrennial Homeland Security Review Report: A Strategic Framework for a Secure Homeland.* Washington, DC: DHS, February 2010.

———. *Reference Manual to Mitigate Potential Terrorist Attacks against Buildings.* 2nd ed. FEMA-426/BIPS-06. Washington, DC: DHS, October 2011.

U.S. Department of Justice (DOJ), Office of Justice Programs (OJP). "CCTV: Constant Cameras Track Violators." *National Institute of Justice (NIJ) Journal*, no. 249 (July 2003): 16–23.

U.S. Mission Geneva. "Press Briefing by DHS Secretary Napolitano and IATA Director-General Bisignani." January 22, 2010. https://geneva.usmission.gov/2010/01/23/ napolitano-bisignani/.

U.S. National Commission on Terrorist Attacks Upon the United States (9/11 Commission). *The 9/11 Commission Report.* Washington, DC: U.S. Government Printing Office, July 22, 2004.

U.S. National Counterterrorism Center (NCTC). *2011 NCTC Report on Counterterrorism.* Washington, DC: NCTC, March 2012.

U.S. Transportation Security Administration (TSA). "Global Strategies." August 28, 2013. http://www.tsa.gov/stakeholders/global-strategies.

——— "Transit Security Grant Program." March 31, 2014. http://www.tsa.gov /stakeholders/transit-security-grant-program-4.

———."Transportation Security Fees," December, 2014. http://www.tsa.gov/stakeholders/historical-fee-collection-data

Wechsler, Harry. *Reliable Face Recognition Methods*. New York: Springer, 2007

Wright, Stephen. "Were They Inspired by Al Qaeda Magazine? Authorities Investigating Whether Terrorists Were Spurred Into Action by Publication Which Urges 'Lone Wolf' Attacks." *MailOnline*, May 22, 2013. http://www.dailymail.co.uk/news/ article-2329337/Woolwich-attack-Were-inspired-Al-Qaeda-magazine-Authorities-investigating-terrorists-spurred-action-publication-urges-lone-wolf-attacks.html#ixzz2vqaSdeYK.

Young Turks, The. "X-Ray Van Sees Through Homes." YouTube video, 5:51. October 1, 2010. http://www.youtube.com/watch?v=SZ2YW7-4Gbw.

Zygband, Patrice, and Hervé Collignon. "The Sports Market." *A.T. Kearney*. May 2011. http://www.atkearney.com/paper/-/asset_publisher/dVxv4Hz2h8bS/content/the-sports-market/10192.